The 5 Seasons of Connection to Your Child

LEANNE KABAT

The 5 Seasons o
Leading Your Fa

ISBN Number 978-1-7335410-7-7

Cover design by NewBreed.Design
Interior design by Ekow Addai
Published by Leanne Kabat Media
Printed by Gorham Printing,
Centralia WA,
United States of America

For current content and event info,
please visit www.5seasonsofconnection.com

The 5 Seasons of Connection to Your Child

More Praise for The 5 Seasons of Connection to Your Child

Leanne's ability to share stories and create teachable moments is magic. Her wisdom is only outshined by her heart. If you are a parent who has ever worried you're doing it all wrong (or if you're like most of us and feel this #everydamnday), this book is for you. Leanne's writing is as beautiful as her lessons are profound. You will walk away from this book with clarity around your family's core values, a new sense of power in parenting, and a deeper understanding of how beautiful imperfection in parenting can be.

Sara Dean,
Host of The Shameless Mom Academy Podcast
(https://shamelessmom.com/)

This book! What a lovely, insightful and truly helpful look at parenting. Her seasonal framework makes all the complexities of family life become easier to handle and brings us back to what's really important: connection and joy.

Amy Lang, MA
Nationally known parent educator
and founder of Birds & Bees & Kids.

I love when I find a kindred spirit, on a similar quest to find more connection and meaning through the journey of motherhood, who realizes that our children have as much if not more to teach us, than we have to learn from them. I've found one in Leanne Kabat, whose book, The 5 Seasons, offers personal reflections and powerful frameworks that shine a light on our parenting path, inviting us to clarify our values, acknowledge the different phases we move through, and bring more mindfulness to how we interact with our children. With honesty, heart and humility, Leanne offers us wisdom and insight from her own experience, so we don't have to move through the seasons of motherhood alone. This is one of those books where you'll find yourself nodding in agreement and excitedly sharing ideas and concepts with your friends.

Julie Neale,
Founder, Coach and Community Builder
at Mother's Quest (www.mothersquest.com)

Contents

Setting the scene

....

M*y life changed in* March 2006. Four months earlier, we moved our family from Ottawa, Canada to Seattle and we were settling into our new life. My husband was away on his first business trip and I stayed home with Alex, who was 4, and Nicole, who was 2. We all climbed into bed around 8pm and being almost five months pregnant, I was happy to fall asleep with them.

In the middle of the night, I woke up to use the bathroom and when I stood up, everything started to spin and I fell down and blacked out. I came to, but I couldn't move and through a tiny slit in my eyes, I could see the clock on my daughter's bedside table. 2am. Then it was 3am. Then 4am. In the hours that I lay paralyzed and frozen on the floor, I asked, negotiated, demanded, and then begged the Universe to give me feeling in my body and be able to move.

Around 7am, a burning sensation erupted in me and everything started to spin, but I could finally move. I woke my kids up and drove to the hospital to check on the baby. That was the first day of an eight-month journey into what caused my brain crash and what I could do to prevent another one. Most days, I was dizzy, forgetful, confused, and very agitated, and when my son was born in July, both the testing and the symptoms increased.

Finally, in November, eight months after the first incident, I met with my medical team and they said they didn't know why I had the crash, or why I spontaneously started to slur, or saw pink neon flashes shooting across my eyes, or had crushing head pain. What they knew, however, was that my brain condition was going to kill me and they advised me to go home, hug my kids, and put my affairs in order. I was given five years to live. I couldn't breathe.

Thursday of the following week was Thanksgiving, and coincidentally my 35th birthday. That day I woke up and sobbed because after dinner, I would only have four more celebrations with my children. In the months that followed, I took all the medications and did all the treatments, but I felt weaker and sicker until 3 years later when I became a shell of a person and a completely disconnected mother. Those years were the darkest times for my family and in no way was I the parent I wanted my kids to remember when they thought of me.

Then, one day, I had a massive wake-up call and with so much conviction and determination, I decided to fight to live. I plunged into self-care in a big way: sleeping all the time, choosing brain-building foods, hiking, practicing deep gratitude and prayer every day. I neglected housework and stopped pretending to have it all together and I dedicated all that time to playing with my kids. I reframed my 5-year expiration to become something to celebrate - I vowed to visit 50 countries before I turned 50, a big goal at the time! As part of my healing journey, I had to find better ways to parent- I didn't want to endure all the stress, the bickering or the fighting that we had in our family before so I came up with games and routines and goals to help us run smoother as a unified team.

I remember in an appointment in 2013, my neurologist showed

me my latest brain scan. Our routine over the past seven years was she would show me the progression of damage from my unknown condition, and I would fall deeper into despair. But this time, I challenged her on what she couldn't see. I told her these scans didn't measure my passion for making a difference. They can't show how I wake up every day full of love for my family, exploring the world through their eyes and giving them new opportunities to see how magnificent their life can be when they stop and smell the roses and meet new people and climb trees and take chances. These scans don't show how I sparkle when I bring joy, laughter, or new ideas to my friends and family. I went on and on until I noticed her wiping away her tears and she said I was her miracle. I laughed, shook my head and replied. No, I was just living in my miracle. My blessed life. Every day was my miracle.

A few years later, I went to visit my sister in Toronto and while she was at work, I had this fire-hose flood of information consume my mind. I quickly grabbed my journal and wrote everything down. From the second my pen touched the paper, I was outlining the 5 Seasons philosophy: organizing the seasons and describing them in detail, sketching charts, brainstorming mini-strategies. I don't know how to explain it other than it was a divine download from God and the Universe to help me be my best even when I wasn't sure what that was. When I had written everything down, I cried. Here it was: a clear, easy way to stay connected in my most important relationships through the ups and downs and ins and outs of our crazy, intense, brilliant, challenging, beautiful life.

I didn't know at the time that the 5 Seasons strategy would

become a way to help others create the family of their dreams too, but I know differently now. Through coaching women for the past few years, I know we can have what we desire when we understand the different seasons and learn how to harness the power of each season to bring out our best and the best in our kids. I've seen families transform from angry to enthusiastic, from controlling to cooperative, from stormy to serene, and from chaotic to connected with some simple but life-changing techniques found in this book.

As you read through *The 5 Seasons of Connection to Your Child*, select the strategies that will make a difference right away, and save the other ones for a time when it will make sense to implement them. Feel free to modify everything to fit your family, there is no one-size fits all in parenting! There will be cool, Fall days, and yes, there will also be Winter storms, but with this newfound framework, I know you can lead your family through the rebirth of Spring towards long, beautiful Summer days.

Sending xoxoxo's for your journey,

Leanne

We often forget our human connectedness.

Throughout my life, I have felt the greatest beauty lies in this connection. It has been in the deepest connections with others that I have experienced the greatest degree of learning, healing and transformation.

This connection is a powerful thing, with the ability to transform lives, and ultimately transform human experience.

~ Kristi Bowman, Author

CHAPTER 1:

Seasons in Parenting

. . . .

When the wind picks up and the autumn leaves swirl, we know what we have to do: put on a warm sweater, grab a coat, and trade in our flip-flops for fuzzy socks and boots. A beautiful summer day means we slip on a t-shirt and shorts to face the world with a smile. We know what a typical day in each season brings . . . which helps us prepare for the day.

But what happens when a cold-snap hits in the middle of our lovely summer?

Or a heat wave in the peak of winter?

Every day millions of people experience bone-chilling cold or heart-melting warmth without leaving their homes.

Welcome to the world of parenting.

Just as nature has its seasons, so does parenthood. Parenting is a study in contradiction: one day you're laughing, playing, and connecting heart to heart. The next day someone is troubled, angry, hurt or frustrated and the family starts swirling in chaos. Dark and stormy moments happen quickly!

Whatever season you are in right now, you are not alone! As a former teacher and mother of three, I've seen the nooks and crannies of all the seasons in hundreds of children and I can guide you through them. Whether your family needs to tweak some things for better connection or is struggling with intense conflict, this book provides a powerful framework to help you be the parent you want to be, bringing true connection and deep love back to your home.

The *5 Seasons of Connection* goes deep to the heart and soul of parenting, right into those crucial minute-by-minute interactions where families draw closer together or pull further apart. If taking your family to a more stable place feels like a dream, have faith.

I can get you there.

Long-term View of Parenting Seasons

To get you started on the right foot, here's a long-term view of seasons every parent experiences to varying degrees:

1. New life beginning with the birth of a baby. (*Spring*)
2. Happy, early years of joy and wonder. (*Summer*)
3. New influence of friends pulls your child away. (*Fall*)
4. Conflict or confrontation peak in teen years. (*Winter*)
5. Your adult child begins his/her own life journey, recognizing your love and care and enters into a new phase of the relationship. (*Spring*)

If you're like me, you don't walk through parenthood thinking two decades ahead. It's lived day by day, hour by hour, sometimes minute by minute.

The 5 Seasons of Connection is designed to help you guide your family from chaos to connection using an easy to remember system of seasons to identify where you are and get you where you want to go in your relationship. Sometimes, figuring out where you are as a parent is uncomfortable, or it unleashes your raging inner critic and you just don't want to go there. It's okay, we'll go there together.

Let me share a story when I came face to face with my less-than-stellar parenting so you can see it happens to all of us. A few years ago, I was doing everything for everyone, especially my three children. I raced through life at warp-speed: planning, shopping, cooking, cleaning, chauffeuring and whatever I could do to meet their needs. Life was so crazy that I kept losing track of important things that made life harder so I came up with a fix. I made lists, dozens a day, for everyone. At night, I wrote reminders for my children and left them on the floor by the bathroom so they'd see the notes and remember their permission slips or a violin or their sack lunch.

Slowly, I started snapping at them more and more. Then barking orders. Then being irritated when they wanted *one more* glass of water at bedtime.

Exhausted, stressed, and living on autopilot as I walked down the hallway one night, I stepped over a pile of papers on the floor.

"Whose papers are on the floor?" I cried. "I need them picked up right now, please."

"I left them for you," my son said.

"I bust my butt for you and how do you repay me?" I snapped. "By being sloppy and ungrateful and leaving messes all over the house? You left them for me? Like I'm your maid? It's your mess, you manage it."

His eyes filled with tears. He shuffled over and hugged my leg. "I'm sorry, Mom," he whispered. "I left you my quizzes to show you how smart I am. Almost all of them were perfect. I thought it would make you happy. I'm sorry it made you so mad. I won't ever do that again."

His papers lay in the exact spot where I left the important notes for my kids.

My heart cracked.

After apologizing, I went to my room, turned on the shower to muffle my sobs, and fell to the floor. Motherhood wasn't supposed to be like this! It wasn't supposed to be so relentless, demanding, and just so damn hard.

How long did you feel confident as a mom?

The first days of being a mom had been a sweet honeymoon phase I loved. With little sleep and less confidence, I adjusted to the rhythms of my tiny baby and learned his different cries, fussy times, super-cute alert times, and saw the world through his eyes. Even though he was running the show, I kept up with him and felt like a great mom.

That lasted a few weeks.

Then my son transformed into a new version of himself. At every stage of development, my parenting had to change. More changed when we added our daughter to the family. After having our last child, let's be totally honest, nothing was remotely the same! But I know some things for sure:

- I'm not the same person I was seventeen years ago.
- My kids have taught me more than I have taught them.

Motherhood can be soul-filling, heart-warming, miracle-making, and life-affirming. It can also be challenging, triggering, exhausting, depleting, and relentlessly overwhelming. We find ourselves at the end of our rope—and yet still willing to sacrifice every last drop to our children.

Then we dig deeper to give even more.

Being the parent we want to be requires complex navigating of some of our most intricate relationships. However our childhood experiences were for us, whether they were stormy or ideal or chaotic, they don't prepare us for our journey as parents. I constantly felt unqualified, overwhelmed, and inadequate. Like many of us, I learned how to parent in the hardest way possible—in the heat of the moment. I know I'm not alone in feeling like I'm failing at doing something that seems like it should all come easily and naturally.

Managing their intense—and often contradictory—needs can push us to the edge of frenzied rage or into a meltdown. When

I first became a mom, I didn't know how to juggle everything expected of me and *not* leave a hot mess in my wake.

What do we want?

To not feel like a terrible mother. To never fail them.

Over the years, I've read dozens of books and talked to hundreds of women about how to be a great mom. Parenting rules aren't set in stone and there isn't a 'one-size-fits-all' guidebook, but I thought I'd find *some* common rules all great parents follow.

I was totally wrong.

Some said spank, some said never. Some said time-outs, some said no. Some swore by strict, rigid rules, some had none.

What was I left with? More questions than answers. But I *knew* that being the parent I wanted to be and having the relationship I dreamed about having would take continuous learning, listening, guiding, and teaching.

The key to that dream would later be found in feeling close and connected. That is something I can help you with.

> *I define connection as the energy that exists between people when they feel seen, heard, and valued; when they can give and receive without judgment; and when they derive sustenance and strength from the relationship.*
>
> ***~ Brené Brown, Author and Thought Leader***

The 5 Seasons of Connection

On my quest for creating the family of my dreams, I found something interesting.

When we were in harmony, everyone was relaxed. We all generously offered help and grace. Inevitably, something would happen and someone in the family would have an outburst. Shouting, crying, or blaming would abound. Maybe someone would shut down and withdraw. The good times were like long, beautiful summer days . . . and then some freak storm would rip through and topple everything.

As I thought about those beautiful summer days, bitter winter storms, spring thaws, and the chill of fall, I saw astonishing parallels to our relationships with our kids and the rhythm of our family. They followed some of the same cycles as nature! From this idea and divine inspiration, I created the *5 Seasons of Connection* framework.

Before I explain these seasons further, let me share a disclaimer.

Four different and distinct seasons don't exist everywhere in the world and if you live along the equatorial belt or close to one of the poles, you may only have two seasons. It's okay, you don't have to live in a four season climate to understand this framework; most of us will have seen movies or shows where seasons are different from our own and we get it. In the *5 Seasons of Connection*, I use the concept of four seasons *symbolically* to illustrate the ever-changing relationship we have with our kids.

Here's a quick overview:

Winter

Winter is the absence of connection.

Here, we feel angry, hurt, disappointed, or unavailable. This season breaks our hearts and hurts our family the most—we want to spend the least amount of time here.

However, we don't want to eliminate Winter completely because it serves a purpose. Winter closes one way of being and makes way for a new way of being in our relationships.

Spring

Spring is the bridge-building stage.

Here we find common ground and invite our kids to reconnect. We listen more and speak less as we find our way back to each other by nurturing kindness and bringing more respect to our interactions.

Summer

Summer is all about loving, connected, open, and respectful interactions.

This is the season we want to spend the most time in while laughing, sharing, and building lasting memories. Our world is bright, our relationships are strong, and the times are memorable. Summer isn't about staying in a fake state of perfection. It means you are your best self while honoring and encouraging your children to be their best selves.

Fall

Fall happens when something cold rushes in—a harsh word, a snarky response, a sharp order, or a rigid, unexplained rule. Here, we start to pull away from each other, leaving a chill in the air and an undesirable distance growing between us.

Crossroads

The fifth season isn't found in the seasonal calendar, but lives in the *5 Seasons of Connection* model. It's called the Crossroads.

The Oxford dictionary defines *crossroad* as: *An intersection of two or more roads. A point at which a crucial decision must be made that will have far-reaching consequences.*[1]

We make a crucial decision at every Crossroad. Do we react with anger or frustration? Do we go into Winter or lead with love and grace back to Summer? Our decisions can create an impact that can be short-lived, or they might linger for days, weeks, or even years.

Children provide us with endless opportunities to stand at the Crossroads. We either choose connection or we choose disconnection.

Did you notice that magical word?

We *choose*.

You might say, "No way, I love my kid! I would never *choose* disconnection!" Well, let's explore that.

Choosing Disconnection

A busy mom named Emily returns home with her car full of groceries. Goodness knows she isn't taking two trips so she loads her arms with bags and shuffles up her front walk. She can barely reach the door because twelve-year old Josie left her bike on the step for the third day in a row. Emily stretches to put her key in the lock and nearly loses her balance when she pushes the door open. She can't feel her fingers because the bags are so heavy. Then she trips on Josie's shoes. Emily is sweaty and annoyed when she drops all the bags. Oh no, there are eggs in one of these bags! She storms off to look for Josie. When she finds her, she unleashes all her built-up frustration. She tells Josie how inconsiderate she is, how hard her morning has been, and how she has been told a million times to put her bike and shoes away. Then Josie yells back, "You win the mean mom award today!"

Whew! Can you feel the stress here?

Without question, our kids *are* responsible for putting away their things. The natural consequences for not doing that fit perfectly here. (Child leaves out bike, child loses bike for a set period of time). We can also make a mental note to teach them to take more personal responsibility like practice putting shoes under the bench over and over until it sticks. However, let's see how Emily chose disconnection in this scenario.

If Emily carried only a few bags to the door and asked Josie to help, she could've noticed the bike and shoes. At that point, she may have calmly reminded Josie of the predetermined consequences of leaving her things out. Josie could tidy up, help with the bags, and share stories from her morning while Emily was out running errands. In this option, Emily would've found herself in Summer.

Alternatively, Emily could have gone inside and simply asked Josie to bring in all the groceries as her contribution to replenishing their food supply, allowing Emily to make a cup of tea and chat with Josie while emptying the bags. This is another good Summer option.

Emily's superhuman attempt to do it all pushed her beyond her threshold, bringing her relationship to a place of conflict and Winter.

Still not sure if you choose disconnection?

Think it just *happens*?

What about when your child comes to your desk, knocks over your coffee, and ruins a very important presentation that you have worked all day to prepare? Your temper flares as you bark at him, "What have you done? My handouts are destroyed! Get out NOW!"

You might think, *that reaction was a bit harsh, but I didn't choose to explode. It was automatic.*

Let's replace one word.

What about when your **boss** comes to your desk, knocks over your coffee, and ruins a very important presentation that you have worked all day to prepare?

In the second scenario, you likely would have said it was all right, jumped up to clean the spill, and kept your temper under wraps. Even in the heat of the moment, you can choose your response.

Choosing differently isn't a gift granted to parents who've had a decade or more of practice. Even as brand-new parents, we've had experience being an adult. We can learn how to bring more love into our interactions using the *5 Seasons* philosophy no matter how long we have been parents. Our children rely on us to bring light into our interactions, guide them with grace, and welcome them into Summer—especially when they're fighting, defying, sassing, and pushing every button we have.

Now let's talk about the individual seasons, and how *you* can choose to navigate them and reach your highest parenting dreams and expectations.

CHAPTER 2

Winter

....

H*ave you ever been* outside in the deepest part of winter, in the darkest time of the night, and simply listened?

Winter has its own heartbeat.

The songs of birds or buzzing of insects doesn't fill the air, like in summer. Winter is hollow and muffled, with bitter winds howling through barren trees. Winter can be downright harsh: severely cold temperatures, bone-chilling winds, early darkness, and the fewest hours of daylight.

I want to explain Winter first because this season is where we feel the most powerless and overwhelmed.

We're emotionally frozen and enduring the darkest times.

A heaviness fills the air when you're together.

Bitter phrases are mumbled and muffled.

The hurtful words hang in the air like our frosty breath.

What is Winter?

In Winter, parents feel:

- Angry, frustrated, hurt

- Uninterested in being around your kids
- Dread when they return home
- Unwilling to share about your day
- Irritation at all infractions, (i.e. leaving dishes out)
- Unsociable with your friends/coworkers
- Unable to do family projects without yelling or rage

In Winter, children feel:

- Feelings ranging from unhappiness to rage with you
- Offended when you share helpful ideas
- You'd be the last person they would turn to for help
- Disengaged
- Closed in mindset and body language
- Embarrassed by you in public
- Unwilling to help with house projects
- Likely to sabotage things at home
- Avoiding you around the house
- Uninterested in family activities

Just like winter looks different in various areas of the world, in *The 5 Seasons of Connection*, Winter shows up differently in each family, and often changes as you move through different life stages. Winter with a newborn is totally different than Winter with a teenager.

For some, Winter is a time of:

- Confrontation
- Yelling

- Screaming
- Sarcasm
- Insults
- Disrespect
- Disobedience
- The silent treatment
- Passive aggressive digs

For other families, the harshest Winters may include:

- Mocking
- Swearing
- Fear tactics
- Threats
- Hitting
- Shaking
- Pinching
- Overly harsh punishments
- Hurtful physical contact

This second list is intense—but these behaviors happen, often peaking during the teenage years. I have met with many parents who felt crippling shame for resorting to an extreme behavior or two on this list when their child pushed buttons the parents didn't even know they had.

Let's talk more about hot buttons.

Hot Buttons

Hot buttons are topics or issues that are emotionally charged, such as:

- Bullying
- Cheating
- Defiance
- Disobedience
- Disrespect
- Experimenting with drugs/sex
- Failing grades
- Issues around food
- Laziness
- Lying
- Quitting something
- Sibling squabbling
- Sloppiness
- Stealing

Why do our kids push our buttons to begin with?

Some children push our hot buttons accidentally or unintentionally while trying to get their own needs met. For others, lighting a fire under us gets our undivided attention because they feel they aren't getting it any other way. Other children push our buttons with the hope that we'll give into their demands and let them have their way.

Hot buttons typically come down to one thing: attention. One way to defuse a possible hot button situation from bubbling up is to invest dedicated attention in your child and understand his current needs. Just like Benjamin Franklin said of fire safety, and countless others say about your health, an ounce of prevention is worth a pound of cure.

If your family is slipping into Winter and attention isn't the main issue, what other possibilities exist?

What Brings You to Winter?

Let's think about a time when your interaction with your child ended in anger, frustration, tears, exasperation, or despair.

Try to recall how it started, continued, and ended. Most likely, you'll recall all the ways your child pushed your relationship into Winter but I'd like you to reflect on the questions below. Think about what triggered *you* to unleash a Winter storm in your home.

1. Did you make decisions and expect total obedience?
2. Did you say things that added fuel to the fire?
3. Could your directions have been misunderstood but you assumed your child was being defiant?
4. Did you push your child away with name-calling, shaming, or mocking?
5. Were your expectations too high? Too vague?
6. Did your body language convey anger and mistrust?
7. Was your volume louder than usual?
8. Was your tone sharp and pointed?

Just like winter is a time of deep physical darkness, Winter with our children is a time of deep emotional darkness. It's here where we face the hard parts of parenting— regulating our own emotions so we don't overreact and escalate issues based on our own personal baggage, practicing self-control in the heat of the moment, and taking responsibility for our contributions to the conflict.

The truth is, we don't come to parenthood with a blank slate. We arrive with:

- A decade (or two) of learning the rules as children ourselves.
- Practice navigating our teen years, enduring our parent's styles.
- Years of stressing, stumbling and succeeding as young adults.

Without question, we come to parenting with baggage and memories—both joyous and miserable. We may come with pain or unspeakable trauma. We come with triggers. Intense emotions can be unexpectedly unleashed in heated conversations with our kids.

The first step out of our frosty darkness is to understand anger.

The Myth of Anger

Anger is a powerful and frequently misunderstood emotion that is blamed for negative feelings and behaviors, particularly when expressed in a destructive or aggressive way. However, anger is a normal part of being human and is important to our experiences.

It acts as an internal alarm and signals that something isn't right.

When you find yourself becoming angry, think about the root cause. Anger is often the mask that covers up deeper feelings like fear, pain, shame, or injustice. Ask yourself these questions:

1. What is the feeling at the root of my reaction?
2. Does my anger help me explore my root feeling or does it mask it?
3. Is there anything in my control I can change?

Sometimes the feelings just get too much to handle and we have to release some hot emotions. You could use some tried-and-true anger management techniques like removing yourself from the situation, engaging in strenuous exercise, journaling your feelings, participating in talk therapy, or meditating. If you decide to feel angry, be angry, and act angry, remember your child is watching. They will learn to manage their own anger based on how you manage yours. If you opt to lash out at another person, and that person fights back, you've now turned anger into conflict.

Mastering Conflict Matters

There is a saying, *How you do anything is how you do everything.*

In *The 5 Seasons of Connection*, how you handle conflict is how you handle parenting because, let's be real, our kids test us.

Over and over and over.

In the same old ways.

In brand new ways.

In ways that stop us in our tracks and take us to the edge.

If we can learn to master conflict, we are empowered to master everything else. Anger defines the emotion, but conflict defines the interaction.

Stormy Weather and Conflict

When stormy weather rolls through our family, we feel it immediately. Most storms come in the form of a disagreement, a struggle, or a clash that arises out of competing opinions. These can feel heavy, emotional, and personal.[i]

I'm going to be honest: When there is conflict with my children, my instinct is to fix it yesterday.

I grew up in a family of intense chaos. Conflict often led to rage, suffering, and pain. It makes sense that I want to sprinkle fairy dust and glitter to make it go away. As an adult, I know that is unhealthy, unhelpful, and ultimately unfair to my kids. They need to learn how to navigate all interactions, from positive ones to negative ones, so I've worked hard to understand the *who, what, when and how* of anger and conflict. This section explores some things I have taught them to feel empowered and secure in emotionally stormy weather.

When we think about the family we've created, we should ask these questions: Do we know how to stay connected during the

---

i Sadly, some adults grew up traumatized by the darkest side of family conflict when their parents wrestled with addictions, violence, abuse, illness, or poverty. In these toxic environments, the damage runs deep into their core. If this was your experience, I am so sorry, and I encourage you to seek support for healing and releasing the pain that burns inside. Your experiences are a part of you, but they don't define you. You define you.

good times *and* the bad? Is our family riding the roller coaster of connected-disconnected-connected-disconnected over and over? Does someone rise up during conflict to drive the outcome, either positively or negatively?

With those in mind, let's explore what conflict means to you.

Your Beliefs About Conflict

Answer these questions about when you were a child:

1. How did your family handle differences or challenges?
2. In times of crisis, were you the recipient of rage/volatility?
3. Did you endure the silent treatment when conflict arose?
4. Did you easily bring issues to your parents to handle?
5. Was there denial? If conflict was ignored, it didn't exist?
6. Did your family play blame-games if things went wrong?
7. Did your family deal with issues/problems as a team?
8. Did someone have to win every argument?
9. Did someone *give in* to bring peace to the family?
10. Did your family brainstorm ideas to find the best solution?

Your childhood experience will flavor your parenting journey and impact your behavior in challenging times because we instinctually go back to what we know when we are in fight-flight-freeze mode. For much of my childhood, I saw that anger and conflict were toxic and damaging so even as an adult, at the first signs of trouble, I jumped into unhealthy responses planted in my formative years.

After years of dedicated research and some therapy, I'm here to say you don't have to be afraid of conflict.

When handled in a mature, responsible way, conflict can benefit your relationship because it:

- Brings simmering issues to the surface.
- Generates healthy conversation/problem solving.
- Allows for new ideas from different points of view.
- Increases our understanding of issues.
- Provides the emotional energy or motivation to implement a solution.

When conflict is handled poorly, however, it becomes a problem.

When Conflict is Handled Poorly

Here are a few examples from parents in my coaching practice who talked about times when they said conflict could've been managed better.

> "She was jumping on me, grabbing and pinching my arm trying to get close to me because she missed me. Instead of pulling her closer, I pushed her off and told her to leave me alone because I wasn't ready to be mauled."

> "I was impatient and pushing her to make a quick decision when she didn't really understand her

choices, but I didn't take the time to explain. She exploded and then I exploded at her for exploding at me."

"Traffic was terrible and he was talking nonstop—even shrieking at some points—and I could barely concentrate. So I told him to shut up or we were going to die."

"She asked to buy three tubes of paint and I just yelled at her. 'Why don't you start taking care of your supplies? I shouldn't have to buy you more because you're careless and let your paint dry out.' She was angry and slammed her door and then I saw a paper on the counter where she signed up to bring in three tubes of paint for the class art project."

When conflict is handled poorly, we say and do things we later regret because we're pushed or pulled in too many directions, with too many competing needs for our time, attention, or energy or we don't have the right tools on hand.

So how do we handle conflict well? When you know yourself, your limits, and your needs, you can step back and see *the whole picture.*

The Whole Picture

Conflict often arises because we don't see everything, we magnify the thing that shocked us out of autopilot living, like a snarky comment, angry defiance, a rude response, a slammed door, or some other form of disrespect. When we hear that rude comment, for example, we don't see the whole picture so if we can remember to pause, turn on the floodlights, and see the whole picture, we might find there are other factors that we didn't initially see.

For example:

- Is your child hungry?
- Overly hot or cold?
- Feeling sick or coming down with something?
- Worried, anxious, stressed?
- Feeling vulnerable or unsafe?
- Dissatisfied in their performance in school/sports?
- Experiencing shame for a mistake they made?
- Struggling with academics or friendships?
- If they are older, could it be hormones?
- Relationship struggles?
- Exam overwhelm?

Seeing the whole picture isn't always easy because there's never one simple cause for Winter. It's a perfect storm of emotions, expectations, and contributing factors. In an ideal world, we'd evaluate every situation from a bird's eye view, but parenting *isn't* perfect. Sometimes as parents we are barely hanging on by a thread. We're on edge and we hear one thing that sends us into reaction-mode.

Zara considered herself a pretty normal parent with a pretty normal child but last week, 6 year-old Anya came home from school behaving in ways Zara called "bratty, whiny, and a bit mean." In every instance of this new behavior, she reminded Anya to speak in her big-girl voice, ask politely for things, and use her manners but it didn't help, Anya continued to behave the same way. Zara made an appointment with her daughter's teacher and discovered that Anya has been so obsessed with getting out to play four-square at lunch recess that she takes a few bites of her food and then tosses the rest so she can be first in line to go out. It was a lightbulb moment for Zara. She would've never thought it was hunger and thirst driving her daughter's behavior. The teacher agreed to set the rule that children had to sit for 15 minutes before lining up, giving Anya time to eat.

When Zara was focusing on Anya's behavior and asking her to use her manners, she wasn't getting to the root of the issue, she wasn't seeing the whole picture. When that happens, and we're stuck on one small part of the whole issue, we're Spotlighting.

Spotlighting

Have you ever been to a theater production or a concert?

Think about the deep, dark stage. The orchestra swells. The curtains rise. A thin spotlight creates a perfect circle on the black stage. The audience is silent until you hear footsteps. Into the spotlight appears a single performer illuminated by the stream of light. You see her face, her hair, and the top part of her shimmering dress. She stands in the spotlight and sings. After a mesmerizing moment, all the stage lights burst on. Dozens of people, tons of props, and an entire set fills the stage. You didn't see any of it a moment before because of the spotlight.

With that in mind, let's go back to one of your Winter interactions with your child.

Did you spotlight?

Did you focus on one small thing and ignore everything else, or not see the whole picture?

In times of conflict, people develop tunnel vision. We're unable to see other possibilities besides the one in our mind. A mom named Mary told me about a time she spotlighted and caused a massive conflict with her daughter.

> One night Mary was expecting her 17-year-old daughter to come home from her boyfriend Steven's house before her curfew, but Kiara was late. Mary waited five minutes, ten minutes, and then fifteen minutes. She called her daughter, but it went to voicemail and there were no texts. She was starting to panic, Kiara was always a few minutes early so her mom wouldn't worry. Finally, twenty-five minutes past curfew, the door opened, and Kiara walked in. Dirt caked her jeans and her hair was falling out of her ponytail and she tried to speak but Mary yelled over her and didn't give

Kiara a chance to respond. After a string of rapid-fire accusations, she grounded Kiara. Mary fell into a kitchen chair and cried. This normally calm mother was rattled all night with fears that Kiara was following in Mary's footsteps of being a young, single mother with a surprise baby to totally change the course of her life.

In the early morning, the doorbell rang. Mary opened the door to find Steven's mother holding Kiara's phone and a bouquet of flowers. Before Mary could speak, the woman said, "Good morning Mary, I hope I didn't wake you. I just wanted to drop off these things for Kiara."

"Oh, thanks," Mary said, "but what are the flowers for?"

"Kiara didn't tell you about our crazy night last night? We were watching a movie but then Steven threw up! I stopped the movie, got Steven to the bathroom and I rushed Kiara to the car so he wouldn't be alone too long. On our way, my front tire blew out! That's when we realized we both left our phones in my kitchen. Neither of us had a phone to call for help. Poor Steven was at home throwing up. It was awful! Anyway, sweet Kiara flagged down a man who helped us change the tire. Once he finished, we raced here because she was panicked about coming home late and I told her I'd bring her phone first thing in the morning. I hope you weren't too worried!"

Mary's guilt crushed her. She had unleashed her fear without any facts, any information, or any flood lights on the rest of the scene. Mary had done more than spotlight—she'd created the deepest, darkest storm of their relationship. Something beyond Winter.

This is called a blizzard.

Beware of the Blizzard

A blizzard is one of the harshest storms in nature, with heavy snow, brutal winds, low temperatures, and extremely limited visibility.

You experience a blizzard when your emotions drown out other thoughts and feelings for a short period of time. Blizzards often occur when severe fear grips us, or long-suppressed memories (conscious denial) or long-repressed memories (subconscious denial) of suffering surface. Since we are the sum of every single thought, action, interaction, feeling, and experience we've ever had, we carry every trouble, triumph, sadness, and success in our cells. These can surface and create a blizzard after months, years, or even decades.

These life experiences could have stayed Winter conditions except for how deeply they impacted you at one time or another. When something rattled you as a child, it stays in your subconscious and can resurface when your child triggers that memory through their own behaviors many years later.

What are some examples where parents have experienced blizzards?

Your child's teacher calls to discuss your child being caught cheating. (Triggers the shame when you were rightfully/ wrongfully accused of cheating in your life).

Your child's coach calls to inform you that your child was caught bullying. (Triggers the fear and horror when you were bullied and humiliated).

Your child steals medication from your house to use or give to others. (Triggers the fear of your child becoming addicted and all the social/physical/relational consequences because you either can imagine the worst or you were profoundly impacted by someone with severe addictions).

Your child has sexually explicit material, either magazines or digital pornography. (Triggers shame around how sexuality was handled in your household, in your religious organizations, or at school. For many, it can also trigger experiences of abuse or sexual violence throughout their lives).

Blizzards will be different for every person because we each bring our own occurrences, beliefs, values and secrets to our parenting journey which shape our relationships significantly. What may be a blizzard for one parent could be a Winter condition for another, but there's no denying the force and severity of a blizzard in your family.

How do you get through a blizzard?

When a blizzard hits your community, you hunker down and focus on the essential things: safety, heat, light. When a blizzard hits your family, you need to do the same and focus on emotional safety, emotional warmth (connection), emotional light (hope).

How do you find those things?

You look inside.

The more in touch you are with your own feelings, emotions, triggers and beliefs, the faster the blizzard will pass.

The blizzard is like a neon-sign flashing relentlessly, it wants you to see it. This may be uncomfortable for you but when you are ready to peel back some of the layers of your feelings and experiences, you may be surprised what you find. Women have shared that when they bravely dive into the most honest and vulnerable feeling that unleashed the blizzard in their relationship with their child, they remember the core hurt, the moment of shame or humiliation, the story of their darkest night of the soul, the thing that nearly ruined their life, their deepest pain – that is what lives in the eye of the storm. It isn't about the curfew, the spilled milk, the failing grade, the snarky response, the potty accident, or any of the endless possibilities that we experience with our kids, it's about who we are and what is inside of us shaping us at our most foundational level.

Some parents push the whole bad experience out of sight, out of mind. That delays the inevitable—you will experience those emotions and their intensity another time. The underlying triggers still exist.

To honor yourself after the blizzard, you'll need to walk through the emotions again and incorporate strategies to help you on your journey, including meditation, journaling, or counseling. Some people can do this deep, inner work alone but many need support and time and there is power in knowing you aren't alone.

Keep in mind—even if you've never experienced a blizzard, your child still might.

Blizzards in Children

As parents, we work tirelessly to give our children a better life than we had. Most of the time we're able to keep them away from traumatic experiences . . . but sometimes horrible things happen. Their experience and the way they emotionally process the event determines if it's Winter or a blizzard. As parents, we don't get to put their events in a hierarchy of importance for them.

A child's blizzard is a tsunami of emotion triggered by a fear that can paralyze them with panic or rage. When they are completely flooded by their feelings, it is their blizzard. For those children who experience it, they need help and support to process and release those heavy, dark stormy emotions.

The first step is to wait it out, just like in an actual blizzard. You can't repair your garden in a storm. After the incident, when their heart rate returns to normal and the rage has subsided, you can ask your child open-ended questions like:

1. Where did you feel this first in your body?
2. What were some of your thoughts and feelings right before the blizzard?

3. In your blizzard, what are some of the things you think about?
4. What kept circling in your mind?
5. How would you like me to help you if it happens again?

By hearing your child's feelings, you may be able to identify some of their fears and work toward uncovering the root cause. To move out of Winter, your response after her blizzard needs to be anchored in the unshakable belief that you love, cherish, and honor her as a worthy and treasured person. They are separate from their behavior.

Spotlighting and blizzards aren't the only responses that push us deeper into Winter.

Let's highlight a few more.

For every minute you are angry,
you lose sixty seconds of happiness.
~ Ralph Waldo Emerson, Philosopher and Poet

Yelling

When your child does what children do (poke, push, press, test, etc.) and your reaction is yelling, you will absolutely stay in Winter.

You tower over them and raise your volume and intensity and they undoubtedly feel afraid. In the beginning, they may apologize or cry so you stop yelling, but over time they become numb to it. Eventually, more yelling—with the added zest of threats or punishment—will be required to get your child to obey. Your child also learns that yelling is an acceptable and powerful strategy for getting what they want, often practicing on siblings or friends.

Interrupting, Assuming, Rushing

Constantly interrupting is a control tactic. Rushing your child to finish her thoughts so you can jump in is another way we keep our family in Winter. Children are not fully skilled at putting all the most important information at the beginning of their sentences. Interrupting them means you may never hear what they think or feel because they don't get all the words out. Without an opportunity for full expression, they lose trust that you really care about their feelings.

Authoritarian Parenting

This parent demands obedience.

They use threats or shame to enforce good behavior. Typically, children can't live up to these unrealistic expectations and are further punished or shamed. The Latin root for punishment is *poena,* meaning pain and penalty. The actions of this parent aren't to discipline or teach, it's to coerce compliance and get control over the child. This parenting strategy will lead to a very long Winter with your child.

Overpampering

Being completely available and doing everything for your kids is not a goal to pursue. Overpampering stunts their developing independence, removes their practice for evaluating and taking age-appropriate risks, doesn't allow them to learn from their mistakes, and prevents them from getting in touch with their own needs and advocating for themselves. When you overpamper, you train your child to wait to be rescued. The day they aren't rescued, their anger will erupt from a place of fear and feelings of incompetence.

Snarky Comebacks

Countless studies have found that rudeness or incivility spreads almost virally[2], much like the common cold in a kindergarten classroom. People who encountered snarky behavior, sarcasm, or general rudeness will suffer in two ways. First, the recipient will have a difficult time managing their impulses, which will push them into reaction mode. Second, they were very likely to be snarky, sarcastic, or rude to another person, perpetuating the chain of negative interactions. It doesn't matter who starts it, but it has the potential of ping-ponging back and forth, hurting feelings, getting personal, and making Winter last a long time for families.

Name-calling

When a parent insults their child, it has a profound effect.

Children of every age crave their parents' approval. When the person they hold in the highest esteem calls them a name, they can feel crushed for days, months, or a lifetime. They internalize these negative names and labels and those become their inner critic which relentlessly judges and shames them.

Favoritism

If you have more than one child, they may all believe there's a favorite in the family. Wintry days will come if you perpetuate that belief through your actions.

Some examples of favoritism include a parent preferring a same-gender child, or being more lenient towards the agreeable, happy child and being stricter with the strong-willed child. Consciously or unconsciously, favoritism can result in one child receiving more attention, more affection, more privileges, and less severe discipline. One major consequence of favoritism is the rise of sibling rivalry. Nothing pushes families into Winter faster than jealousy, competition, and fighting between siblings.

Sibling Rivalry

Sibling rivalry is not about the sibling, per se. More often, it's about one child's fear that her uniqueness, status in the family, or attention from the parents is being threatened by another.

Some ways that *persistent* sibling rivalry keeps us in Winter include:

1. Treating everyone equally

The desire to treat everyone equally stems from the hope that when everyone feels equal, they will get along. This disregards the fact that everyone doesn't need the same thing. If Christy falls and scrapes her knee, does everyone need a bandage? If Adam wins first place, do all siblings get a medal?

Instead of equality, strive for *fairness*.

For example, let's say you ask your seventeen-year-old son to drive his sister to baseball twice a week, mow the lawn on the weekend, and empty the dishwasher after school. But you ask your ten-year-old daughter to take care of the cat. If you were treating them equally, they would both receive twenty dollars per month and sibling rivalry would plague your family. Your son would probably feel overworked and undervalued. If you were treating them both *fairly*, your son would receive twenty dollars and your daughter might receive four dollars. If she wanted more, she could help more around the house.

2. Making Everyone Share Everything

A recent mantra seems to be, "share, share, share!"

But not allowing kids to set their own personal boundaries around their toys can make them feel powerless, jealous, and keep them in Winter. When your four-year-old receives a brand-new remote-control car and has played with it for mere minutes before having to give it to his little brother for his turn, sibling rivalry will emerge. It's important to teach them that sharing builds relationships and allows others to have experiences they might not have, but it's also vital to allow them their own item for a certain amount of time.

3. Enforcing Rules Willy-Nilly

When you create a set of rules but only enforce them sometimes, or they only apply to some children, it keeps sibling rivalry alive and well.

If your rule is, *you hit, you sit,* and your littlest one hits but doesn't sit, your other children will be angry. If your rule is, *homework before television,* but you let your middle schooler watch a show on her iPod when she gets home from school, your boys will be angry she gets screen time and jealous that she found a loophole.

4. Force Them to Hug and Make Up When They're Still Seething

If your kids erupt, give them physical and emotional space to cool off. They will most likely stay in Winter or create an even bigger storm if you have them sit and hash it out right away. Instead, separate the kids and let them regain their composure before talking about it, taking responsibility, and coming up with a plan to avoid a similar conflict in the future.

5. Ignoring Their Need for 1:1 Time

All kids need different things at different times.

As a parent, meeting each child's needs is challenging, especially if you have more than two children. However, spending high quality, uninterrupted time with each child is one of the best strategies to combat sibling rivalry. Ultimately, your children want more time with *you*. Carving out time for each child will strengthen your family dynamics.

When You're Ready to Leave Winter

Winter can last a very short time, or it can plague us for what seems like forever. Sometimes I consult with parents who've been in

Winter for weeks because they had forgotten they had the power to leave. Winter has a way of keeping the negative emotions swirling.

Think of it like this: one day snow falls (conflict occurs) but doesn't melt because the temperatures stay below freezing (issue isn't solved). No new snow falls, but a sharp wind keeps stirring up the fallen snow . . . thus creating an endless Winter. As it sometimes happens, we can stay in Winter because one conflict keeps whirling around with disconnection and hurt.

In Winter, reflecting on how our children's behavior contributed in the interaction is important, but the cold, dark reality means it's time to reflect on our behavior.

Some parents say that Winter feels too harsh and too uncomfortable. We should do everything in our power to avoid it at all costs. But Winter serves critical purposes for our family.

First, it escalates a problem that has not received the attention it deserves. Second, it gives your children a chance to be brutally honest and show their hidden feelings when something is amiss. Third, the brutal winds blow away dying habits or old patterns so new habits can form in the next season. We don't want to remove Winter! Instead, we strive to reduce the frequency, duration, and intensity of this crucial season.

We are not broken.

Our kids are not broken.

In moments of hurt, fear, or in times when we are triggered, our worries and weaknesses rise to the surface. We put up our defenses and operate in survival mode—but we shouldn't stay.

When we're ready to come from a place of love and connection, we are ready for Spring.

> *Even if today may seem to be a time of total darkness, it will not last forever. The dawn will surely come if you advance, ever forward, without being defeated. The day will come when you can look back fondly and declare, "I am savoring this happiness because I struggled back then." It is those who know the bitterness of winter that can savor the true joy of spring.*
>
> ***~ Daisaku Ikeda, Author***

CHAPTER 3

Spring

....

Spring is the season of new beginnings.

After a harsh winter, spring brings cleansing rains to wash away the heaviness. It welcomes lightness, possibility, hope, and renewal. In *The 5 Seasons of Connection*, Spring brings all those feelings into our relationships with our children.

What is Spring?

Spring is beautiful and fresh and hopeful. It's the bridge between Winter and Summer.

In Spring, we feel:

- Free from the physical/emotional weight of Winter.
- Able to be on offense instead of staying on defense.
- Happy to enjoy small moments with smiles, laughter.
- The strength to offer forgiveness for past hurts.
- Less friction during conversations and less reactivity.
- Patience and grace, which leads to listening, learning.
- Open to express thoughts, needs, and feelings.
- Confident to ask, *Where are you going? When will you be home?*

In Spring, our children feel:

- Free to be out of their room and spend time with you.
- Less afraid of yelling, nagging, other Winter conditions.
- More open to conversation, sharing a story.
- Agreeable to playing a game, doing something together.
- Interested in joining the family for dinner.
- Willing to help around the house, complete chores.

Sometimes your child will be the one to reach out by telling you a story about her day, asking a question, requesting a snack, or bringing you something from school. Often, you will be the one making the first move. You may choose to smile and thaw the emotional freeze, or reconnect in a welcoming, meaningful way.

This season is complex because we're coming out of the most disconnected time (Winter) and moving towards the most connected time (Summer), so Spring bridges us from emotional heaviness to happiness. As we cross this bridge, we'll explore one essential focus: Spring Cleaning.

It's time for a spring cleaning of your thoughts,
it's time to stop just existing, it's time to start living.

~ Steve Maraboli, Author

Spring Cleaning

There's something cathartic about clearing away the buildup and debris and preparing for the promise of warm days and fresh air.

In *The 5 Seasons of Connection*, Spring Cleaning provides a critical transition toward warmer interactions and fresher connections. Just like you can't tackle your whole house all at once, you can't tackle this whole season at the same time either. A thorough deep cleaning happens in phases.

I break it down into two sections: internal and external.

Internal Spring Cleaning

Our first commitment to step fully into Spring is to fill our cups first. That way we can replenish what Winter may have taken away. That means investing in ourselves. We discover what we need to learn and where we are now in our relationships with our children.

There are two main practices for Internal Spring Cleaning: Journaling and Self-Care.

Internal Spring Cleaning: Journaling

Journaling is one of the most powerful ways to Spring Clean your mind, spirit, and prepare you to reconnect. This practice has the potential to rise above all others on your Spring journey because it's where you get real, honest, and vulnerable with yourself.

There are no rules for journaling. You can make it as simple or as fancy as you'd like, but the key is to write as raw, as unedited, and as honestly as you can. Be consistent. Give yourself permission to get intimately involved in a relationship with your true self.

How you do it is up to you. Some people record their first thoughts every morning for a few moments before they check email, wake the kids, and start their day. Some journal at bedtime. Either way, you can write in a stream of consciousness about your thoughts, or bullet-point things that went well, struggles you encountered, and successes you experienced. (No matter how big or small.) There are the dedicated few who journal morning *and* night.

On the pages of your journal, you are the author and the audience. Only you will see those pages, so you can remove the mask of perfection and be authentically, unapologetically you.

Record your thoughts, feelings, fears, wishes, hopes, and dreams for yourself, your children, and your family. See where you are today and where you want to go. This seemingly simple practice helped me form my sense of identity as a woman and as a mother. The more honest I became, the deeper I could go to heal old hurts, offload baggage, and create the life I wanted.

Other superpowers that arise from journaling:

1. Journaling can reveal you exactly as you are, not distorted from years of other people's criticisms, judgments, or limiting beliefs. You have the power to understand the true you, see the things you do very well or the parts of you that need time to become stronger or wiser. Writing honestly about yourself strengthens your sense of self.
2. Journaling helps you wade through the murky waters of an unpleasant encounter. It brings clarity and compassion. When you find yourself in an intensely emotional state, journaling can help you experience and understand the full spectrum of your feelings. When you have a negative interaction with your child, it's easy to go to a place of hurt,

anger, or fear but journaling allows you to deconstruct the situation, regain your objectivity, and see it from other angles.

3. Journaling can identify patterns over time. It will show you the places you keep going to when you're triggered or feeling out of control. When you read over your past entries and see the same themes, you can consciously untangle them and be empowered to change.
4. Journaling gives you permission to dream. It clarifies your hopes, wishes for your family, what you want to experience, and how you want to live. Then it gives you the opportunity to brainstorm more ideas to keep moving you towards your ideal life.
5. Journaling tracks how far you've come. Over time, you'll see where you were, where you are now, and all that you have overcome on your journey so far.
6. Journaling, when combined with gratitude, changes lives. When you write down all that you're grateful for, you change your outlook from scarcity to abundance.
7. Journaling strengthens your relationships when you write about who you love. Things like why you love them, what you appreciate about them, their strengths, and how they make you feel, plus cute memories, funny stories, shared moments of tenderness, random acts of kindness, and memorable instances. Bookmark these in your journal! Reading past entries about my love and appreciation for my children helped me return to Spring and Summer when

a storm was brewing or Winter was on its way.

Think of journaling this way: it's like that time in summer when you collected extra berries to make jam. Jam isn't exactly the same as the fresh fruit but tasting it can take you back to those great days when you picked them fresh in the sun. Your journal can take you back to the best moments with your child.

Journaling is extra effort in a busy and demanding day, I know. We are moms, wives, sisters, daughters, employees, entrepreneurs, miracle-makers and life-changers – we are busy people! However, a commitment to journaling is a commitment to your personal growth unlike many other methods.

Although journaling has immense power to move you towards Summer, knowing who you are and *where* you are in your parenting journey will help you recognize and implement other vital self-care practices.

Let's talk about self-care next.

> *Self-care is never a selfish act - it is simply good stewardship of the only gift I have, the gift I was put on earth to offer others. Anytime we can listen to true self and give the care it requires, we do it not only for ourselves, but for the many others whose lives we touch.*
>
> **~ *Parker Palmer, Author***

Internal Spring Cleaning: Self-Care = Self-Love

Self-care has become a media buzzword—but it isn't about massages and manicures, nor is it new-age or woo-woo. True self-care is about being the healthiest version of ourselves and boosting our sense of well-being.

We may have descended into Winter for many reasons, but one common factor that contributes to countless Winter experiences is depleting our spiritual, emotional, or physical reserves below the healthy limit. When we live to give it all away as a parent, partner, or person in our work environment or community without nourishing ourselves, we risk going back to Winter personally, which brings our relationships with our kids back into Winter too.

Self-care can take many forms, but ultimately when we invest in self-care, we are choosing to honor and cherish our whole selves-spiritually, emotionally, physically, relationally, intellectually, and occupationally. Strong self-care practices nourish us, and as a result they allow us to guide our families into Spring, modeling healthy life habits along the way.

One challenge many parents face is deeming self-care a luxury. When faced with choices on how to allocate time, energy or money, women in particular will opt to cut out self-care. When this is the case, then we have to face the reality that women place other people's well-being above their own. Oftentimes, when this happens, it is either an issue having a low sense of self-worth or we lack clearly defined boundaries.

Setting and Upholding Firm Boundaries

What exactly are boundaries?

Boundaries are emotional, spiritual or physical limits we put in place to communicate how we want to be treated, what we will accept, what we will tolerate, and what is not welcome in our relationships.

Examples of weak boundaries with our kids include:

- Accepting rude behavior without correction
- Doing child's project for him when he's struggling
- Putting your child as the center of the family
- Oversharing burdens or problems with your child
- Giving your child authority to drive your decisions
- Living vicariously through your child's struggles and successes, making his experiences your own

Try this exercise to help you set personal boundaries so you stay in Spring and reconnect with your child.

1. Identify a situation you felt disempowered, stifled, wronged, or resentful.
2. Create a rule that re-establishes your parental power in that situation and share it with your child, with clear expectations and desired outcomes.
3. Consistently enforce that rule with your child.
4. Follow through on consequence when rules are broken

This Spring Cleaning activity is challenging for parents who crave connection with their kids at any cost because they feel that giving in is good relationship-building. However, when your kids see your boundaries are more like swinging saloon doors and less like bank vault doors, their behavior changes to include whining, screaming, or physical aggression - not any behaviors that you want.

For example, Alicia has a rule that her family is to leave all areas tidy and clean. Every day, eight-year-old Sonia makes her snack and then goes out to play, leaving empty wrappers and crumbs on the counter. Alicia grumbles but cleans it up and sometimes makes a snarky comment at dinner.

Now that Alicia is reevaluating her boundaries in Spring Cleaning mode, she can meet Sonia in the kitchen after school. She'll tell Sonia she's happy that she makes snacks for herself, but she can't play until the area is clean. If Alicia has to call her back to clean her mess, Sonia will get an extra chore after dinner.

> "The first day was fine, Sonia took care of everything. Day two, three, and four though were rough! Each day I had to call her back in, endure tons of tears and tantrums for what seemed like hours, but finally Sonia realized this boundary was here to stay and she didn't test it anymore. I've been very soft on having boundaries because a part of me wanted her to like me, but we feel closer now that there are firm rules in place."
>
> ***~ Alicia, mom of Sonia***

Reaffirming your healthy boundaries will model a few vital lessons for your child: the importance of knowing how they would like to be treated in their relationships, that they are their own people with responsibility for their thoughts, feelings and behaviors, and that healthy boundaries help them connect in an authentic way. Strong boundaries serve as the foundation for investing in self-care practices that transform your life and your sense of well-being.

Are Well-being and Self-care the Same Thing?

Well-being is an all-encompassing term that assesses your health, happiness, feelings of fulfillment, and enough-ness in your life. Self-care practices, on the other hand, are the things you do to nurture your well-being. If your self-care practices are lacking, your sense of well-being will be low.

When we neglect self-care, we feel:

- Exhausted
- Burnt out
- Unfocussed
- Short-tempered
- Inefficient
- Disorganized
- Impatient
- Stressed out
- Sluggish
- Stuck

We often don't realize we've treated self-care like *a luxury we can do without* until we make choices that contribute to our decline.

Huge deadline? Just skip breakfast to get it done.

PTA meeting? Grab a protein shake and call it dinner.

Sick kiddo? Sleep is overrated.

Stressed out? Eat mindlessly until it's wine o'clock.

Penelope knows this cycle all too well. She shared this story about the price she paid for ignoring her body:

> "When Stella was born, her needs always came first, of course. I started dividing my time between her and my husband. Next baby, I divided my time into three. It was that way for years. You could look for days but you wouldn't find me doing anything for myself. I was so stressed, suffering from headaches, just mentally unclear and super anxious about little things. I snapped at everyone, even a delivery guy who tried to be funny. I kept giving and giving until I felt like I was just the shell of a person.
>
> Then one day I collapsed at the mall and ended up in the hospital with adrenal burnout syndrome. The doctor asked me if I would ever let my child's health decline for eight months and ignore it.
>
> "No, of course not!" I replied.
>
> She responded, "So then you are just less worthy?"

It was a shot in the heart and I was speechless. I thought being the best mom was constantly giving myself to everyone, but there were two problems.

First, I ran dry. I had nothing left to give because I never refilled my own cup. Second, I modelled for my daughters that to be a woman or a mom, you must give and give until there isn't a drop left. That is not how I want them to think about motherhood, wife-hood, employee-hood, or anything else.

I want them to nurture their passions and find hobbies that fill them up, but I didn't do that for me. From then on, I modelled healthy mind, body, soul, and family balance. Everyone is happier for it."

~ Penelope, mom of two

There will never be a time when the flight attendant tells you to run around the plane and put everyone else's oxygen mask on first. Giving your kids the best of your time, energy, and spirit requires you to come to the interaction full, nourished, and ready to share your heart. It cannot be done if you're exhausted, burnt out, feeling disempowered, neglected, or depleted. We often guide our kids to get more sleep, eat more veggies, play more outside, and hang out with kind, compassionate people because those are basics for building up their self-care habits, however we don't follow our own great advice. We take on too much, work too hard, tolerate too often, and over-give too many times, hurting our own sense of well-being. We don't need to prove we're good moms by powering through at all costs. We need to commit to investing in our own well-being and prioritize excellent self-care practices so we can fully arrive in Spring and welcome our children with us.

When the well's dry, we know the worth of water.
~ Benjamin Franklin, Inventor, Author

Let's check in on how you are taking care of yourself:

Self-Care Quiz

Y	N	Do you have a morning routine that centers you before your busy day?
Y	N	Do you eat healthy, nutritious food?
Y	N	Do you allow yourself to feel uncomfortable feelings without stuffing them down or numbing to them?
Y	N	Do you exercise three times a week and move your body most days?
Y	N	Do you sleep 6-8 hours a night?
Y	N	Do you have work or projects that stimulate your mind and grow your skills?
Y	N	Do you spend quality, uninterrupted time with your partner?
Y	N	Do you feel confident that you're managing your money well?
Y	N	Do you spend time on hobbies or personal interests?
Y	N	Do you say no when you need to step back from commitments?
Y	N	Do you have friends who really understand you?
Y	N	Do you use your talents to contribute in a fulfilling way?
Y	N	Do you meditate, pray, or calm your thoughts and emotions regularly?
Y	N	Do you ask friends for help when you need it?
Y	N	Do you have a nighttime routine that allows you to release the stresses of your day and settle down and prepare for sleep?

Scoring

_____ Yes answers _____ No answers

11-15 YES answers: Congratulations! You have prioritized self-care and you know it's a critical part of your wellness practice. You are in the best place to model self-nurturing practices for your kids.

6-10 YES answers: You have some good self-nurturing practices and you're on your way to healthy and vibrant living. Once you're ready, add another practice or two to keep your whole self nurtured.

1-5 YES answers: Oh my friend, I'm going to be honest... let's put you at the top of your to-do list asap! You put everyone else's needs above your own, which means you neglect or deny yourself time, nourishment, and investment to stay healthy and strong. You are at risk of being in your own personal Winter.

Purposeful and meaningful self-care is the cornerstone of our lives. Those who invest in themselves by taking active care of their needs can reach more of their goals, meet the needs of others better, and achieve a higher feeling of well-being and feel more fulfilled when reflecting on their lives.

Is All Self-care Equal?

The short answer is no.

Some self-care practices will be more essential or have greater consequences at a given time. Overall, you'll need to assess and invest in all sections of your personal well-being for optimal health, happiness, and vitality.

How do you know what sections of your personal well-being need attention? There's a wheel for that!

The Well-being Wheel

This wheel identifies the six unique sections that contribute to our overall sense of well-being. If one or more of these categories are lacking, we can't reach our highest potential of health, happiness, or vitality.

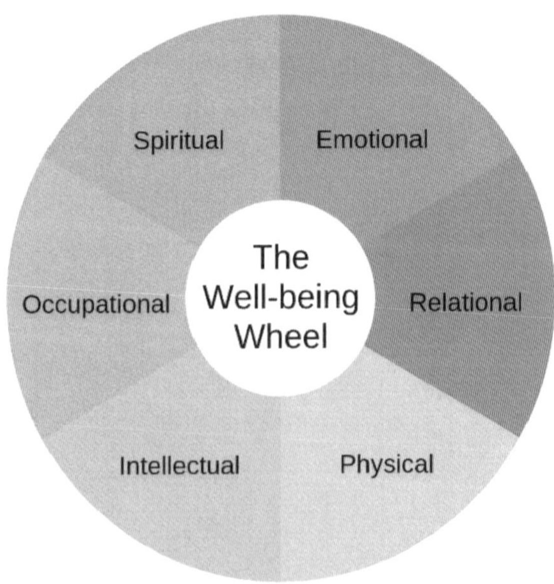

Spiritual[ii] -meaning, quiet, purpose, prayer, meditation
Emotional - feeling all the feelings, the good and the bad
Relational - strong bonds with kids, partner, friends
Physical - food, sleep, activity, stress, health checkups
Intellectual -learning, manage resources: money, time
Occupational[iii] - using your talents and skills in work

At a glance, you might feel pretty good about nurturing all these parts of yourself, but if you're coming into Spring after a particularly harsh Winter, there will be some self-care practices that could use some TLC.

But which ones?

The following chart helps us check in with our true feelings. It's very simple to complete but holds profound value for our life. There is absolutely no shame in the well-being game so be honest with yourself.

The first time Kay did this exercise, she filled all the categories to the top and proudly showed how she was honoring herself and making self-care a priority. I asked if she would be willing to share how she practices self-care in one or two of the categories. She stared for a second and then tears sprang into her eyes.

---

ii Spirituality is often interchanged with religion, but you can be deeply spiritual in nature, in meditation, in service without a religious component. Either way is perfectly fine.

iii *Occupational* self-care refers to our marketable skills that we can use outside our family and home responsibilities to perform paid work, start a business, write a book, or volunteer in some capacity.

"When I held up my chart showing that I was awesome, no one saw that I was hiding behind a mask. When Leanne asked if I would be willing to inspire others, it shook me to my core. My true self, under my mask, is a woman spiritually tired, angry, bored, lonely and fed-up. I couldn't lie to these women. I cried, releasing the pain and shame of neglecting my body, mind, and spirit in my effort to be the *perfect mom/wife/woman*. I did the chart again. It looked nothing like the first one but was a true and accurate reflection of my self-care. It gave me a new place to start building something real."

~ Kay, mom of four

For each category, on a scale of 0-10, shade how full, how nurtured, and nourished you feel.

- 0 is the lowest (I neglect myself completely)
- 3 is low-ish (I try to practice a few things a month).
- 5 is medium (I practice something every week)
- 7 is high-ish (I do a few things around 3x/week)
- 10 is the highest (I've a daily practice that works)

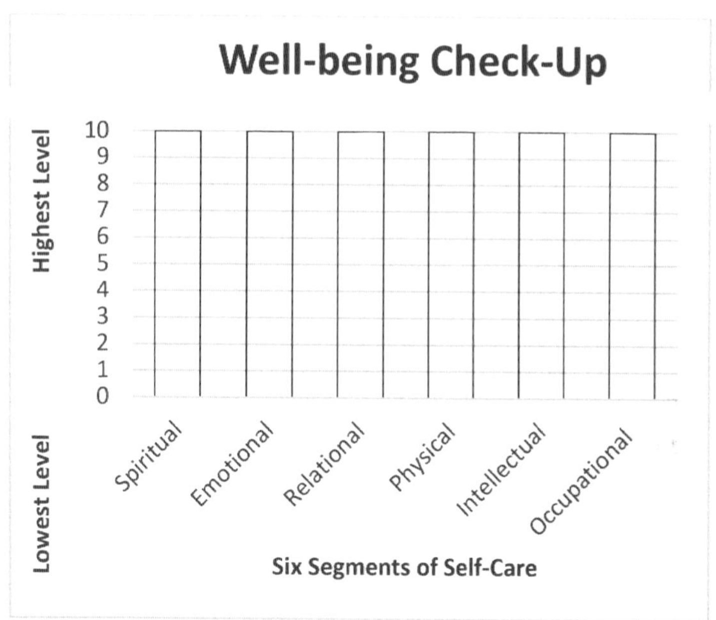

Did you uncover some surprises?

Before we work through this exercise in coaching sessions or in group settings, many women feel their self-care practice is decent and could use a little fine-tuning. After we've completed it, when they see how low they've scored, it's a true wake-up call!

Many of us need to get serious about investing in ourselves on all levels.

How to Nourish the Six Sections of Well-being

If you scored low in any way, here are a few helpful ideas:

Spiritual

- Walk in fresh air. Listen to sounds around you.
- Light a fire and be mesmerized by the flames.

- Lay on a blanket at night, watch the night sky.
- Walk barefoot in the grass.
- Meditate on your own or with a guided program.
- Attend the house of worship for your religion.
- Pray or speak what's in your heart.
- Practice random acts-of-kindness.
- Read inspirational/religious texts for hope.
- Soothe yourself near water— a river, lake, or ocean.
- Practice mindfulness by focusing on simple items
- Find the miracles in your day, big and small, and be thankful in the moment.

Emotional

- Journal without censoring, editing, restricting ideas.
- Watch for hot button triggers, respond differently.
- Set /maintain firm boundaries on your time, energy.
- Practice gratitude each day by recognizing five gifts.
- Watch your negative self-talk, quiet your inner critic.
- Say yes to your needs. You matter very much!
- Allow your pet to be a source of emotional support.
- Feel your big emotions, remember you're in control.
- Allow yourself time to create art, cook, sing, dance.
- Schedule white space in your day and simply *be*.
- Spot your *numb-out* ways (eating, shopping, drinking) and practice staying with the feeling instead.
- Limit time on social media, avoiding *highlight reels.*

Relational

- Schedule 1:1 time with each child. Be fully present.
- Have date nights. Talk about everything but the kids.
- Spend quality time with people you love the most.
- Be around people who positively impact you.
- Volunteer in your community.
- Nurture some close, trusted friendships.
- Thank someone who positively impacted your life.
- Find a new hobby that involves other people. (Hello introverts! This is for you!)
- Call a good friend and check in with them.
- Send a post-card to a loved one when you travel.
- Organize family activities that are simple and fun.

Physical

- Stay current on your medical/dental checkups.
- Commit to drinking more water.
- Plan and prepare healthy meals and snacks.
- Commit to exercising or being active every day.
- Protect your sleeping time ferociously.
- Substitute sugar foods with natural treats and drinks.
- Sign up for lessons in a new activity, like pickleball.
- Put scented oils/salts in bath as a stress reducer.
- Explore creative movement with dance/flow exercise
- When you need to cry, laugh, scream, vent – do it.
- Make time for playing active games with your kids.
- Stretch to gently strengthen/lengthen your muscles.

Intellectual

- Explore an art gallery. Learn more about the artists.
- Visit a museum, research the history of the pieces.
- Turn off the news, disconnect devices, and just think.
- Work on a crossword puzzle or Sudoku.
- Take a class.
- Watch a tutorial online for a DIY project.
- Say no when you mean no.
- Say yes when you mean yes.
- Read. A lot.
- Learn a new musical instrument.
- Limit tabloid-type-TV and watch documentaries.
- Use lists or apps to stay organized and productive.
- Surround yourself with smart, thoughtful visionaries.

Occupational

- Balance your work and life demands.
- Create a healthy space with vital items within reach.
- Find a mentor or be a mentor.
- Problem-solve to maximize your sense of control.
- Take classes to improve your skills for more income.
- Network with people in a field you are interested in.
- Deepen your skills that bring you to expert status.
- Take assessments to identify skills, talents, passions.
- Start a small business.
- Know your industry and stay current in your market.
- Lead projects at work/gain new skills as volunteer

- Especially for stay-at-home-moms—take a skills inventory and know your worth.

My Self-Care Plan

Now that we've brainstormed some ideas, take a moment and fill out this chart. Commit to adding a few new self-care practices to your day and week.

Don't feel pressure to put huge, complicated items on your list. Instead, think of ways you could support your overall health and happiness that fit easily into your life, such as reading an inspirational passage first thing in the morning, drinking a glass of water before your coffee, taking the stairs, turning off your phone after dinner, scheduling a date night once a month, or meeting a friend for a walk.[iv]

You can use this chart as a way to commit and track new practices. This is a *practice*. It isn't perfect. Celebrate every step, no matter how small or sporadic, as you begin your self-care journey.

---

iv For those of us who struggle with self-worth: seek the support you need. When we hide, hibernate, or isolate ourselves too long, we forget how powerful it is to connect with other women and mothers to normalize the 'hard' and get some fresh perspectives from an outside point of view. There is power in sharing stories from the trenches, whether it be breastfeeding breakdowns, toddler tantrums, partner problems, or teen troubles. Your friends can help you through Fall and Winter times so much better than you can get through them on your own. Trust. Connect. Accept friend love.

Self-Care	I will add...	When ready, I'll add...
Spiritual		
Emotional		
Physical		
Relational		
Intellectual		
Occupational		

Your Child's Self Care Plan

Now that you have explored your self-care situation and put new practices into place, it's equally important to gently support your child doing the same. Some families focus solely on the Spiritual-Emotional-Physical-Relational categories, adding in the others as the child ages. If you aren't sure what goes on their self-care plan, just ask them!

Here are a few suggestions:

> Honey, what brings you joy when you are sad?
> What makes you smile when you are feeling ho-hum?
> What would you do all the time if you could?

Many of the strategies to nourish your well-being and increase your self-care may also work for your children. However, here are a few more that are child-specific and age-appropriate.[v]

Additional Ideas

Spiritual

- Swing at the park and feel the wind in their hair.
- Blow bubbles and watch them float away.
- Watch the clouds roll through the sky.
- Listen to music that brings happiness and joy.

Emotional

- Use art to nurture self-expression.
- Read or write poetry.
- Take pictures of cool things around your house.
- Make a scrapbook/ journal to explore feelings.

Physical

- Go on a bike ride through your neighborhood.
- Have a bubble bath.
- Play with your pet.
- Plant seeds in a starter kit or a garden.

---

v I keep costs for self-care practices down by going to the dollar store, the clearance section of other stores, and our online Buy Nothing group, but honestly, many of our practices are no-cost.

Relational

- Invent a new game for your family to play.
- Watch a show together and talk about it.
- Play charades or other acting games.
- Read a story or a chapter together before bed.

Intellectual

- Design and build a fort in your house.
- Plan a tea party with invitations, tea and snacks.
- Find a dessert recipe and bake it together.
- Research a cool science experiment, conduct it.

Self-Care	One practice your child can add
Spiritual	
Emotional	
Physical	
Relational	
Intellectual	
Occupational	

Walking into Spring when everyone in your family has invested in their well-being allows you to release the heaviness of Winter. This creates a new feedback loop that spirals upwards: you will take care of your needs, you will feel more open and receptive. Your child will take care of his needs, he will feel open and receptive. And on and on. As you both feel better and more centered, you can reconnect.

Spring Cleaning takes time and effort, but once you've finished one section, you're ready to move onto the next.

Now that we've taken care of our Internal Spring Cleaning with journaling and self-care, it's time to move onto our External Spring Cleaning, which focuses on our interactions with our children.

External Spring Cleaning:

Once we have completed a thorough cleaning of our habits, practices, and behaviors, we need to spend time investing in shifting our relationships to a place of warmth and openness.

External Spring Cleaning covers three important areas:

1. Apologizing and Forgiveness
2. Peace Plan
3. Family Systems

External Spring Cleaning: Apologies & Forgiveness

Apologies

Every family will find their own way to reconnect after a cold, dark Winter season. For many adults, the idea of apologizing, forgiving, and moving forward is new. For others it's unfathomable. Some parents in my program have laughed out loud at the idea, saying, "I'm the boss. I will never have anything to apologize for!" and "I will not be weak in front of my child, or he will walk all over me."

I get it.

Admitting to being wrong or doing wrong isn't easy, especially when dealing with kids: they have no authority, they can't fight back, and their vocabulary and self-awareness are limited.

But not being easy is no excuse.

It's critical that we use apologizing to firmly plant our feet in Spring and use it as a teachable moment to reflect on an interaction and take responsibility for our participation.

Whether you started the initial conflict or joined into your child's rage parade, you can apologize for your part in the process. As part of this conversation, you are not telling/asking/expecting them to apologize. You are apologizing because you participated in the conflict. Now, you are modelling the way back into Spring.

Sometimes, your child will apologize right after you. Sometimes they need more time to process. In nature, some seeds sprout quickly, and some germinate. We don't fault the seeds that need more time to sprout—we patiently wait. That is our role with our children as well.

Three Components of a Powerful Apology

Good apologies include three main components.

1. Acknowledgement
2. Reflection
3. Commitment to change

Let's run through an example, say you're very late picking your child up from school.

First, you acknowledge your role in the situation. (I left work too late.)

Second, you reflect on why you chose the way you did. (I really wanted to get my report completed and I lost track of time.)

Third, share that you empathize with their point of view and state what you could do differently next time. (From now on, I will set the alarm on my phone so that I leave on time. If I'm not finished my report, I will work on it at home or after your bedtime because being on time to pick you up is very important to me).

This example was pretty clear-cut, so let's explore other scenarios parents face and think about the role of apologizing. What if you yelled because they wouldn't stop pushing your hot buttons? What if you promised to play with them but did something else instead? What if you lost your patience because they were taking too long?

For all of these examples, absolutely apologize. There are very few parents who have never raised their voice, forgotten a promise, or lost their patience. Each of those situations are opportunities for you to express regret and share ideas of what you could do differently next time. Martha found herself feeling awful one night when five-year old Tara wanted a glass of water, then a different story at bedtime, then her other doll, then a nightlight, then her pillow fluffed, and when she asked for another glass of water, Martha snapped. We worked on this script as one way to apologize (though it could be said countless ways):

"I'm sorry I yelled at you. It wasn't kind or loving. I got frustrated because I didn't expect you to want so many new things tonight. It sounds like we could add a few more items to your bedtime checklist, which means coming to bed a bit earlier to get everything done. Shall we work on that tomorrow after school?"

This apology framework works with our older kids as well.

One teen shared that his mom was always yelling at him. She responded that she yelled because he never listened – a lose-lose situation. In private, I asked the mom if next time her son pointed out that she was always yelling, she could respond differently.

"You're right," she might say. "I'm yelling a lot and I certainly wouldn't like someone to speak to me that way. I'm sorry. I need to manage my frustrations better."

She reported back to me that she did use this script. At first, he was speechless, then he said, "I'd be frustrated too if I asked someone to take out the trash and they didn't and now we have to keep it in the bin rotting for another week. Mom, I'm sorry. I said I would do it and I didn't. I'll do it before school from now on."

By showing her child that everyone makes mistakes (by yelling) and accepting responsibility to find new ways to respond (will handle frustrations differently), this mom kept her relationship in Spring. She taught her son how apologizing can heal patterns of disconnection and as a bonus, he has a new life skill.

Forgiveness

Apologizing and forgiveness are two sides of the same coin.

Apologizing is an expression of remorse for doing something that causes hurt to another person. Forgiveness is pardoning someone else for something hurtful that has been done to you. Psychologists generally define forgiveness as *a conscious, deliberate decision to release feelings of resentment toward a person or group who has harmed you, regardless of whether they actually deserve your forgiveness.*[3]

This isn't about *if* the offender deserves your forgiveness.

True forgiveness isn't about the other person, it's about you. The act of forgiving frees you from toxic, boiling rage. Only then are you able to move forward.

Some people live their whole lives holding onto past hurt, pain, and trauma. As new hurts arise, they add it to their heavy heart, deepening their own pain and suffering. Many will actually suffer physical manifestations of their pain, such as higher blood pressure, higher stress hormones, decreased sleep, increased depression, and more incidents of aches and pains.[4]

To be fully in Spring with your child, you will need to choose to forgive her for her hurtful act, destructive words, or reckless behavior. There is no value in holding onto your hurt and *punishing* your child by choosing not to forgive. In all actuality, your child might quickly forget the incident and wonder why you're distant and cold. By talking to her about the incident and forgiving her, you're teaching her that being connected in a good relationship is more important than being right, bitter or vengeful.

The weak can never forgive.
Forgiveness is the attribute of the strong.
~ Mahatma Gandhi, Civil Rights Leader

External Spring Cleaning: Peace Plan

One of the gifts of Spring is the opportunity to see things from a fresh perspective. It's the celebration of the start of something new—like a healthier way to deal with interpersonal differences.

That's why we're going to discuss the Peace Plan.

When you use a Peace Plan to talk about natural consequences, you give your child a better understanding of what is at stake when introducing conflict into the relationship.

A Peace Plan is your family's strategy to work through conflict or disagreements in a healthy and respectful way. There are a number of ways you can detail how your family will work through challenges. Here are some Peace Plan ideas from other families:

1. They identify a step-by-step process for what happens when conflict or disagreements occur, like removing yourself from the situation, asking questions to better understand the other person's point of view, asking for help, or setting a timer so each person has the same few minutes to express their point of view.
2. They outline the family rules and as it becomes age-appropriate, the whole family meets to set the consequences for bending/breaking those rules. Experts recommend the children propose the consequences, not the parents. When the children drive the process, they're more invested in following the rule. Conversely, if they break the rule, they aren't typically screaming about how unfair it is because they chose it.

3. They use role playing to explore their feelings in a safe, non-confrontational way.

Let's look at this last one a little closer since it might be new to you.

In the performance, you be the child, your child is the parent. In your scene, you should break a rule: take something without asking, use your phone more than your allowed time, avoid your homework, etc ... (feel free to use something relevant to your family). As you gently and skillfully push the *parent's* buttons, watch how your child handles it. This exercise not only puts your child in a power position so he can see how it feels to be the *parent* of a *child* (you) who exhibits defiant or disobedient behavior, but it also puts you in the submissive position so you can see how your child might feel powerless with you at times. All of these feelings are great connection points for conversation afterwards. (As the adult, be on the lookout that your child feels safe and the role-playing is age- and developmentally-appropriate to avoid hurt feelings or overwhelm.)

When you have a solid Peace Plan in place, a strategy to turn to when conflict arises, your family is better able to get through it with feelings valued and boundaries respected. Your Peace Plan allows you to focus on connecting, not correcting, to stay in Spring.

Creating Your Peace Plan:

Communicate to Connect, Not Correct

Communicating to connect sets the intention that the outcome of your interaction is to preserve the relationship. This is where you lead with love.

The following framework is helpful for any challenging parent-child interactions when the child is old enough to take turns speaking and listening and can express her point of view. We have used a modified version of this with children as young as four years old.

The goal is to create a set of rules to manage conflict in a healthy way. If an issue or challenge happens, come together and work through this process to keep your relationship intact.

1. Discuss one issue at a time. If another issue arises, write it down for another time (no kitchen-sinking, which is talking about everything including the kitchen sink!) This also helps you stay in the present and not bring up issues from last week or last year.
2. Use I-messages to state the problem clearly and avoid blame. "I feel hurt when you don't put your dish and cup in the dishwasher after dinner," instead of, "You're so selfish to go watch TV, leaving me to slave in the kitchen every night."
3. Take turns speaking calmly and listening. No yelling. No interrupting. No plotting your response. Listen to understand. You can repeat key phrases to avoid misunderstandings, but the only questions you should ask are to clarify the current story, not to lead the discussion down a different path.

4. Brainstorm solutions. Be open to compromising for a solution that works for both parties. Conflicts aren't solved if one person gives in so the other person gets her way. Find common ground and strive for a win-win.

Some issues have no easy answers. There will be decisions where some people won't get their way, but even then you can stay in Spring by turning on the floodlights, seeing as much of the whole picture as possible, and negotiating the best outcome for everyone.

What if your face-to-face interactions get heated and you feel you might slide back into Fall or Winter?

We can reduce the intensity of our interactions by using a tool like a communication journal.

Communication Journal

As mentioned before, parents come with baggage of our own.

Triggering conversations push our hot buttons and throw us into Fall or Winter. We may need a little space to work through them—thinking about alternative forms of communication can increase our chances of staying in Spring. Communication journals can get our thoughts across without the pressure of instant feedback through facial, body, or verbal cues.

How does it work?

It's really simple. You write to your child in a dedicated journal about your thoughts, feelings, or point of view about an incident.

You can consider answering these questions:

1. What I saw ...
2. What it made me feel ...
3. I made the decisions I did because ...
4. The fears or worries I had included ...
5. Some ideas to resolve it includes ...

When you are done, leave it for your child to read and respond with her feelings and interpretations. Taking away the intensity of a face-to-face interaction often allows our children to write more thoughtful, fully expressed ideas about their deeper feelings.

These journal entries often reveal the things our kids are craving most, such as a deeper sense of security or healthier family connections. These can be created by implementing better routines and structures, also known as Family Systems.

External Spring Cleaning: Family Systems

Guiding your family into Spring takes dedication and commitment to your Family Systems. You have to step up and be the parent who nurtures their kids in Spring and Summer while working to avoid Fall and Winter. None of these are ground breaking ideas, but their simplicity holds power. It requires conscious commitment to follow through every single time.

Spring is transitional. The risk of slipping back into Fall or Winter is quite real. If it feels like you're living life in survival mode—rushed, harried, chaotic—it has nothing to do with your love or devotion, and everything to do with the lack of effective Family Systems. By implementing these systems, stressed families become successful, strong, and connected. They bring order, structure, and meaningful practices to your lives.

For children, these Family Systems, also called routines, are critical. Consistent activities and expectations that happen at the same time in the same way provide comfort and a sense of safety. When they are young, routines teach trust and emotional stability.

Think of the systems listed below as gorgeous wildflowers. They all look beautiful, but you don't need every flower to make a stunning bouquet! Select the Family Systems that will keep your family moving toward Summer and put the rest aside for when you need to revisit the list.

System 1: Family Meetings

Without question, this is one of the most powerful systems your family could adopt.

Family meetings are opportunities to bring everyone together and share successes, solve issues, make future plans, update calendars and commitments, set goals, and check on the inner workings of family life.

Many parents open the meeting by sharing a short story and then asking everyone for a personal or a family win from the week.[vi] Then, it's time to get into the business of running your family.

How do you decide what gets on the agenda? If your kids

vi Some families also take a moment for personal or family lows, which helps the parents keep an eye on an unknown blizzard that might be brewing (stress for upcoming tryouts, anxiety over a big exam, a falling out with a good friend) but this isn't the place to dig deeper into those responses. Do that after the meeting in a one-on-one setting.

are younger, you choose one thing to discuss. At this stage, these meetings are meant to show them that working together on issues is part of your family's success.

If they're older, you can put a blank agenda on the fridge so they can add items throughout the week. Some topics we've covered include: screen time limits, delegating chores, defining standards for *clean* rooms, upcoming school events, holiday plans, and cell phone rules. If you're just starting with family meetings, pick non-emotional topics for the first few to practice active listening, problem-solving, and cooperation without unleashing a storm.

Regardless of how old your children are, set basic ground rules for success such as respecting everyone's opinion and keeping it a safe space for people to talk about their feelings without being put down. Limit meeting time to no more than twenty minutes and cover the most urgent issues first, deferring other items if needed.

As your children become more skilled at explaining their problems, finding common ground, listing out pros and cons of various options, and being a part of the solution, the better prepared they will be when conflict arises. The more your family practices this framework of problem-solving, the better they will be at solving problems.

Successful family meetings end with something fun. Many families close the meeting with dessert or an outing to the park. Fun memories reinforce the truth that family meetings help you stay in Spring and move towards Summer.

System 2: Master Your Morning

When you're in Spring, it's critical to start the day with optimism and happiness in your heart.

Your morning sets you up for success. When you're fresh and rested, you're available to help your children start their day. The one thing that *is non-negotiable* is waking up (and actually get up!) at least thirty minutes before your kids.

I know, I know... you might want to give up before we even start but I want you to trust me.

If you're frenetic and panicked in the morning, you'll ooze that energy onto them. They'll ramp up in reaction and that creates the perfect storm faster than your bread can turn to toast.

If you need more sleep one day, honor your body that day. But if you chronically need more sleep, it's time to evaluate your bedtime. If you aren't a morning person, find a few extra wake-up incentives like a quick walk with a buddy (you won't let her down!) or setting a coffee maker timer so you smell the brew.

Your morning routine needs to nourish you and be filled with things that matter. Checking email, social media, and watching the news don't make this list! They put us into reaction mode, disrupt our thoughts, and may force us to reprioritize the day before we've even checked in with our heart.

How do you pick the right things?

Consult the list below—or create your own list—and say, "If I completed these (two, four, six) things, my day would begin from a place of peace and calm."

Morning Routine Ideas

- Breathe deeply for one minute
- Set an intention for the day
- Identify five things you are most grateful for
- Stretch or do yoga
- Exercise vigorously
- Drink water with lemon
- Massage your arms or legs with peppermint oil
- Put on your favorite song and dance
- Shower
- Wash your face
- Eat a healthy breakfast
- Enjoy a piece of fruit
- Make your bed
- Blend a smoothie
- Read from a religious, spiritual, or uplifting book
- Make yourself a cup of coffee or tea
- Review you daily calendar (being open to change)
- Prepare meals for the day

Making a morning routine was never on the to-do list for Chantelle until she noticed she was the angry, resentful mom she never wanted to be.

> "Once I understood *The 5 Seasons of Connection*, I realized my mornings threw us into Winter every day.

A typical day before mastering our morning was insane! Our family of four active kids usually woke up late, then everyone rushed around to find what we needed, my husband was running to the gym, and I come out to find one kid is taking too long to get her cereal so I take over, splashing milk on my pants and then I growl at her and go back to my room to change my whole outfit.

As I'm coming back to the kitchen, another kiddo drops the container of blueberries and they scatter all over the floor. The dog is going nuts as I try to push him away and clean them up, all while ordering the kids to jump in and help. They are busy looking for this paper and that book and those socks and some special sweater no one has seen in two weeks. I peek at my phone and realized I forgot to buy snacks for the youngest kid's class so I grab a box of crackers and hope that's good enough, then rush them out to the car with frantic waving and barking orders. They get to the school out of breath and feeling drained before their day begins.

Now that I've learned these strategies, we are a totally different family. I truly believed it saved my sanity and made me the kind of mom I always dreamed of being!"

~ Chantelle, mom of four

System 3: Master Your Evening Routine

As a natural extension, a successful morning routine is even more powerful for your family if you bundle it with a strong evening routine, including:

- Signing, reviewing, and discussing homework and projects after dinner (not in the morning!).
- Picking out everyone's clothes for the next day
- Putting out bowls, spoons, and dry breakfast foods
- Signing forms or paying fees
- Placing everything in your family's Loading Zone (near the front door, garage door, etc)
- Shower, wash your face, brush your teeth
- Put on fresh pajamas
- Read from a religious, spiritual, or uplifting book
- Journal about your day with highs/lows, funny stories, deep thoughts, ideas.
- Review your calendar for the next day, identify things you need you might not have needed today (phone charger, cash, library books, grocery list, etc.)
- Lead family stretching exercises before bed
- Make lunches, label them, and put them in the fridge
- Fill up water bottles and put them in the fridge
- Share love and sweet moments with each child

System 4: Family Meals

Dozens of surveys show that kids who have dinner with their families do better in every possible way.

According to a University of Michigan report on how children spend their time, family mealtime was the single biggest predictor of academic success. It was more influential than time spent in school, studying, attending religious services, or playing sports.[5]

To plant your renewed relationship firmly in Spring, family meals (which could be breakfast, lunch or dinner) are like a rainbow after a storm – beautiful, delightful, awe-inspiring, and something to share. It isn't about the food itself. Any meal will feed the body but sharing *family* meals feeds the relationship.

It doesn't have to begin at the table. It can begin at the grocery store or farmer's market. Have your kids participate in shopping, preparing, and cooking the meal to create an opportunity to understand how to nourish the body, discover new foods, and share old stories.

System 5: Homework

Although some schools are reducing or removing homework, there will be days when your child will have reading, daily practice worksheets, or special projects to work on at home.

When you want them to work on their homework will depend on your schedule, their extra-curricular activities, how much homework they have, if they're able to get it done on their own, and how well they understand their projects.

They may come home from school, have a snack, and dig into

homework right away, which frees up their time. In another option, they may come home, have a snack, play, relax, and work on homework after dinner. Test different times of the day for each child to help them be successful but having a dedicated homework space could benefit everyone.

What are some features of dedicated homework space?

- A desk/table, chair in a quiet space
- Pens, pencils, crayons, lamp
- Calculator
- Ruler
- Books
- Glue/scissors
- Homework requirements from teacher

Many families slide back into Winter because the child doesn't have these fundamental tools available.

Another key indicator for success is their ability to use a planner to break down larger projects, track deadlines, and complete their work on time. Children who try to remember all the moving parts will struggle. Teach them to write everything down in one place and work systematically toward a small reward, like selecting the song for your dance breaks or choosing the fruits for her smoothie.

Homework has a way of pushing some kids deep into Winter, so help brainstorm ideas for when they are stuck. Do they have a homework buddy? Is there a guide sheet? Can you find videos online that explain the concept?

Ultimately, you know the temperaments, abilities, and rhythms of your children. You are in the best place to set their homework plan to stay in Spring and move toward Summer.

System 6: Make Chores Mandatory

Let's do a fun little activity.

Below, I've listed twenty-five typical family chores. Go through the list and select who typically does each chore.

Chore	Adult task	Child task
Collect/sort/fold laundry		
Pull weeds		
Care for the pet		
Water plants		
Get mail, sort bills/junk		
Sweep the kitchen		
Put away groceries		
Prepare parts of the meals		
Wash the dishes, pans		
Take out the garbage		
Clean bathroom		
Vacuum carpet		
Clean countertops		
Empty/refill dishwasher		
Dust		
Wipe appliances down		
Clean windows		
Mow lawn		
Set table for meals		
Clean out refrigerator		
Organize papers, forms		
Sweep the porch		
Clean out the car		
Tidy entrance		
Match socks		

Are you surprised by how many of these are taken care of by you or your partner? How many do your children do? Every item on that list is attainable for most school-aged children. Children as young as three can toss toys in a bin and can add water to the doggy bowl.

I'm taking a stand here.

When children are given responsibilities and contribute to the flow of the family, they feel empowered, valued, and responsible. In a 2014 survey by Braun Research, 82% of grownups polled said they had regular chores when they were growing up, but only 28% reported asking their children to do any.[6]

In my very *unscientific* poll, many parents reported although they want their kids to help out, they don't insist for a few reasons:

1. They didn't start when their kids were little, now it's too late. (It didn't matter if their kids were six or sixteen, everyone felt it was too late to start).
2. Their kids are so busy with extra activities and homework, they feel their kids don't have the time or energy to help out.
3. They aren't willing to add anything to nag/fight over.

Excluding our kids from family chores leads to parent burnout. That's one of the fastest ways to descend back into Winter! We carry, do, drive, cook, clean, perform, wait, serve, and then BOOM! Our frustration and resentment spills into our relationships and we disconnect.

Kids need to contribute to the ongoing functions and maintenance of the household. Families in Spring and Summer recognize that it takes a lot to run a household smoothly and everyone can contribute in their own way. One mom named Jayna couldn't believe her preschooler was old enough to help when she took over a chore unexpectedly.

> "My daughter is three and won't leave me for a moment. One day I had poured some cleaner into the toilet before I jumped in the shower. She grabbed the toilet brush and scrubbed the bowl the whole time she was waiting for me. She was so proud! When my husband got home, she ran and told him that she cleaned the toilet and she pulled him to the bathroom to show him how it sparkled. Seeing her that proud made me realize that she wants to contribute and feel a part of our team, and after that day, we became a true team of three."
>
> ***~ Jayna, mom of Kallie***

Chores help children learn how to master skills, contribute to their family, be more thoughtful about the impact/messes they make around the house, learn the value of hard work, and practice managing their time and energy. All of those are very important life skills. To build your children's muscles of empathy, caring, and investing in the family unit, the chores should benefit the family, not themselves. Having your child clean the kitchen is more powerful that having your child clean his room.

Many families use time in their family meeting to rotate the chores. One option is this: Every week kids receive three types of chores:

1. A daily chore (dishwasher, set/clear table, sweep)
2. A *Mon/Wed/Sat* chore (trash, tidy bathroom,)
3. A weekly chore (vacuum floors, mow lawn, clean car)

If you're new to chore management, you'll need to:

- Assign age-appropriate/skill-appropriate chores.
- Define the deadline.
- Outline the consequences if the chores aren't done.
- Set your expectations for what *finished* means. (This may take more time for new chores or younger children, but they need to know where to find the supplies, how to properly clean the space, how to safely use the tools required, things to avoid, and how it should look after cleaning.)

Another system that some families find successful is the Chore Zones, which is perfectly suited to older children and teens. I have found that if a child's job is to vacuum, he won't even notice that someone left their socks and sweater on the sofa, so for my family, specific and dedicated chore lists keep them working with tunnel vision. Chore Zones gives them a whole area to maintain for the week. In our family, we have five main zones: main entrance and bathroom, family room and household laundry (towels, tablecloths, etc.), dining room and dining table set-up/clean-up, kitchen sink and counter, kitchen island and floor. Each person gets one zone per week, kids and parents. I have found that for us, having them be responsible for all parts of a small section leads to a cleaner, more stress-free system and I don't freak out anymore that they sat on top of a pile of clean towels left on the dining room chair because their job that week was to sweep the floor.

Systems 7: Screen Time Limits

This is hard to begin with—and gets harder as they age if your child is a tech-fan!

This generation of children doesn't know a time before devices. They often don't even know what a phone book or an atlas even looks like! I've seen one-year-old babies looking at picture books while trying to swipe the pages, as if they are scrolling through a feed.

Nonetheless, tech geniuses Steve Jobs and Bill Gates both denied handheld devices for their own kids until they were teens because they recognized the lure, addictive properties and the dangers of too much screen time. Chris Anderson, CEO of 3D Robotics and a father of five shares the same feelings. "My kids accuse me and my wife of being fascists and overly concerned about tech, and they say that none of their friends have the same rules... That's because we have seen the dangers of technology firsthand. I've seen it in myself, I don't want to see that happen to my kids."[7]

Too much screen time impacts a child's ability to have

conversations, share emotions, and connect with others. They exhibit higher levels of stress and even addiction. Kids who have too much unrestricted time on devices tend to struggle with obesity, irregular and inadequate sleep, loss of social skills, violence, and a loss of active play time.[8] The American Academy of Pediatrics (AAP) has warned that children need to have limits on screen time and it recommends *entertainment* screen time, such as television, movies, videos, video games, and social media, follow these guidelines:

For babies up to 18 months old: Video chatting only (to connect with a traveling parent or a distant relative).

Toddlers 18 to 24 months old: High-quality programming that babies and parents view together.

Preschoolers 2 to 5 years old: No more than one hour a day of high-quality programming, viewed together.

Kids ages 6 and up: No specific time limit. Instead, parents should "place consistent limits on the time spent using media and the types of media, making sure media does not take the place of adequate sleep, physical activity and other behaviors essential to health."[9]

So many parents regret giving their kids unlimited access when they were little because they find themselves in constant battles when they're older. It's easy to increase the limit a bit every few months—but you will unleash a whole world of pain if you give your child too much screen time, then chop it in half.

To ensure quality screen time for your child, research the program/game/app on Common Sense Media or other research-based sites designed to help parents make good choices for their children.

At any age, your child needs supervision when online because searching for the popular toy of the day often brings up results that include adult-only content, even if you install parental controls. Plus, when you're together during screen time, you can explain what they're seeing if it's over their current level of understanding. Many times, children don't get the whole picture. You can use this as an opportunity to talk about issues such as race, gender, bullying, etc.

How do you set limits?

Josefina told me about a strategy which really helped her son understand the need for limits.

> "When Gabriel was 6, we let him have free reign on his iPad because he only used it sporadically, but sometime around the age of 8, he was craving it all the time. When he was using it, he either zoned out completely or became angry or belligerent. He wanted to download some game and it wasn't working. When I looked at his device, I realized he had over 150 apps or games downloaded. It was completely full!
>
> After some research about what to do, we

planned a day to clean it up together. I'm a nutritionist so we talk about food a lot. Healthy food/brain food/body food versus junk food/empty food/sugar food. I created two folders and we sorted every game into its appropriate folder—if it was educational or brain-building, it went into the brain folder. If it was mindless or lacking value, it went into the junk folder. I then gave him a choice: he could play a junk game for 10 mins a day or a brain game for 45 minutes a day.

We set the timer each day and after 2 days of junk game playing, he started to choose the brain games exclusively and we haven't had an issue since. Sometimes he will want longer time, but we have a chart on the fridge that outlines he has to play outside, build something, create something, cook something and clean something, and then he can earn another 15 minutes.

~ Josefina, mom of Gabriel

System 8: Prioritize Books, Music, and Play

I've never found a study that says, "Don't bother reading to your child, it doesn't matter."

It matters *so* much!

Reading builds brain connections, strengthens concentration skills and memory recall, increases vocabulary, teaches social and problem-solving skills, and allows your child to explore feelings through characters in the story without any risk. Reading can also help your child reduce the stress of hard times, an escape into another life and another reality, even for a short period.

For other kids, music offers a space of peace and magic. Listening to music or even creating music is a blessing. Some people dismiss music as frivolous, but studies have proven that music helps children develop language and reasoning skills, stimulates the brain to retain information better, lifts our mood, boosts specific kinds of intelligence, and helps children learn math and complex problem-solving skills. Kids who practice also master memorization at an earlier age, and most get confidence boosts for their achievements.

In every corner of the globe, though, there is one common truth about kids: they learn through play.

All day long, kids are operating in the *adult* world: following rules, speaking a certain way, obeying linear processes, physically looking up to talk to tall people, and feeling very small and powerless. Play is the language of children. When you follow their lead, they grow in confidence and self-worth because, for a short while, they are in control. They decide how you can join and what the rules are for the game.

"The doll sleeps here in the tree ... the truck can only drive there in the river ... the pieces go this way... this is the color you can color the monkey ... this is how you jump on the log."

Children want and need to connect with you in play. It's how they figure out their world. Through games, children effortlessly practice math skills (number recognition, counting, grouping, and patterns), language skills (letter recognition, matching, color recognition and reading) physical skills (hand eye coordination, rolling dice, moving pieces, spinning counters), and social skills (sharing, taking turns, waiting, weighing options and thinking.)

As well as all this, play provides opportunities to practice winning and losing gracefully. Playing card games, board games, or dice games inexpensively provides the perfect framework to practice life skills, keeping your family in Spring and Summer because of a muscle they build called *frustration tolerance.*

Think of a game like Chutes and Ladders.

Your child is diligently going along the path, all smiles, and then BOOM! He lands on a chute and down he goes. His energy drops from 100% to 0%. When our kids face any frustration, it triggers something in us to jump in and problem solve. Please resist! It's time to step back. This is their time to process their feelings and figure out how to feel better. Let them lead.

Allowing them the golden opportunity to self-direct helps them build their frustration tolerance muscle. They will more easily deal with the ups and downs in a low-stakes game so they can be strong enough to flex this muscle when the stakes are higher, like not making the soccer team. When your child feels overwhelmed or frustrated, help her work through it by validating the challenge, showing how ups and downs can happen by chance and are not a reflection of effort or skill, and remind her of when was victorious.

To stay in Spring and move to Summer, you keep going and never give up. You may win, you may not win!

But you always do your best.

Success in Spring

Spring is a powerful season full of possibility and hope.

Nurturing deep, meaningful relationships with our children is more attainable when we set boundaries, establish routines, and nurture and nourish ourselves and our children through targeted self-care practices.

Success in Spring is not about making everything different or becoming a totally new kind of parent. It's about finding what works for you and your family . . . and doing more of it. When you honor yourself and your needs, your children and their needs, and your whole family and its needs, you will most certainly flow right into Summer.

> *We say that flowers return every spring, but that is a lie. It is true that the world is renewed. It is also true that that renewal comes at a price, for even if the flower grows from an ancient vine, the flowers of spring are themselves new to the world, untried and untested. The flower that wilted last year is gone. Petals once fallen are fallen forever. Flowers do not return in the spring, rather they are replaced. It is in this difference between returned and replaced that the price of renewal is paid. And as it is for spring flowers, so it is for us.*
>
> ***~ Daniel Abraham, Author***

CHAPTER 4

Summer

• • • • • • •

Welcome to Summer!

There is no denying the sweetness of this season. Fruits and veggies, at the peak of ripeness, are juicy and full of flavor. The sun shines brilliantly. We're happy, smiling, and socializing outdoors. Beaches and parks are packed with families throwing Frisbees, having picnics, grooving to upbeat music, and enjoying life. We luxuriate in the longest days and the shortest nights, allowing plenty of time to be in a happy place mentally, physically, and emotionally.

Contentment reigns during the Summer—when we finally have the time to enjoy ourselves and those around us. We play, explore, or simply watch the clouds roll through the blue sky.

What is Summer?

Being in Summer with our children is what we crave as parents. It brings a peace and joy that feels like the bright sun warming you to your core. It's your happy place! It's where you go to draw deep inner peace, strength, and profound nourishment to your life and your relationships.

When our relationship is in Summer, we feel:

- Happy to be around our kids
- Excited for them to return home
- Open to sharing *slice of life* stories or childhood tales
- Forgiving of small mistakes like leaving out the milk
- Emotionally present when socializing with friends
- Confident we can work together on a project/chore

When our relationship is in Summer, our children feel:

- Happy to be with us: laughing, listening, sharing
- Interested in your stories and ideas
- Safe to ask for help with something on his mind
- Engaged and open in mindset and body language
- Willing to help with projects around the house

A vibrant and positive energy flows through the family in this season because everyone feels like they're on the same team. Ask any family that's in Summer and they will be the first to reveal that it doesn't happen by accident—you invest and nurture and cultivate your relationship with your child. It was once cold, distant and rocky, but you make it burst with love, laughter, and new growth.

Once you arrive in Summer, you'll have to work to stay here. You'll need to parent with purpose to stay in heart-centered connection with your kids. When you are more mindful of each person's needs, wants, and desires, you will intentionally choose ways to cultivate your relationships with your kids.

Think about it this way: You'd like to grow some vegetables.

You buy the soil and the seeds. Is that all it takes to grow food? Of course not, that's only one step! You work hard to prepare the soil and plant the seeds. Is that enough?

Well, *something* might grow, but likely only a small percentage of what could grow if you tended to your garden. It takes clearing, tilling, regular watering, weeding, sometimes mulching, protecting your garden from pests and other creatures, and sometimes support sticks or extra nutrients to help it reach its full potential. Growing a healthy and vibrant garden takes time and investment.

The same is true for growing your healthy and vibrant family.

Common Traits of Families in Summer

Every family is different. However, the families who spend most of their time in Summer have some common traits. They:

- Honor their core family values daily (more in chpt 9)
- Commit to the happiness and well-being of others.
- Recognize a parent-child hierarchy yet hear each voice.
- Cultivate safety to share emotions without shame/fear.
- Accept that conflicts or disagreements are natural and work together to find the best solutions for the situation.

Why do parents cultivate and nurture those loving relationships with their kids? For many, it's the core mission of a successful and meaningful life.

"Ultimately, the highest salary and the best car aren't fulfilling," says David Niven, author of *100 Simple Secrets of Happy Families: What Scientists Have Learned and How You Can Use It*. "Loving relationships are. They are the foundation of who we are. Happiness isn't what happens to us, it's the love, connections, and support structure we have, and giving of yourself unconditionally."[10]

Happiness

Happiness lives deep in our relationships with our kids.

Much has been written about happiness. Entire organizations are designed to research the science of happiness. According to Dr. Emiliana Simon-Thomas, the science director at The Greater Good Science Center at the University of California, Berkeley, happiness is "the propensity to feel positive emotions, the capacity to recover from negative emotions quickly, and holding a sense of purpose. Happiness is not having a lot of privilege or money. It's not constant pleasure. It's a broader thing: Our ability to connect with others, to have meaningful relationships, to have a community."[11]

It's pretty refreshing to hear that happiness isn't smiling every second with no negative feelings intruding on your cheerful life. Not even close! The science of happiness discovered that happy people have negative things happen all the time but it doesn't knock them down or push them back into Winter.

Why is that?

Happiness is a mindset that helps you rate your life as *mostly good*.

When we train ourselves to see life as mostly good, it doesn't mean everything is perfect, it means we feel confident we can create good things in our life. We know we control our responses and reactions. In the face of a challenge or difficult situation, we know we have everything we need to get through it and come out stronger, wiser, and more resilient. That process helps strengthen our happiness muscle. Then we can model it for our kids so they learn how to live mostly happy, and mostly in Summer.

Some of you might think that you don't have that kind of power. Maybe you're a *glass half empty* kind of person. Your parents may have been pessimists so you feel you're destined to be one as well. Or the shame you carry or the scars you hide prevent you from being happy.

If we were in the car, sitting side by side, I'd stop the car right here. I would turn you to and look into your beautiful eyes and tell you the absolute truth:

You are worthy of happiness because you are you.

You don't need to earn it, justify it, or negotiate for it.

If those words make you uncomfortable, or maybe you scoffed a bit or dismissed my words, I'm going to say it again—you are absolutely worthy of happiness without doing anything at all. All you need to do is choose it because Summer welcomes everyone, genetics or scars or burdens aside!

When you have the mindset that you have the power to choose happiness, you not only change your outlook, but you impact your health as well. People who rate themselves as 'happy' experience:

- Lower heart rate and blood pressure[12]
- Lower risk for heart disease[13]
- A stronger immune system[14]
- Fewer pains with chronic disease[15]

However, one of the most surprising studies showed that happy people impact their body chemistry on a cellular level.

Researchers from Finland studied the emotional reactions of 701 participants across multiple countries and created a body map of where people felt emotions. Of the six primary emotions and the six secondary emotions, happiness is the only one that ignited the whole body and made the most profound impacts on the most parts of our bodies. The next most complete emotion is love. [16]

(Primary emotions are reactions to external events and include: anger, disgust, fear, happiness, sadness, surprise. Secondary emotions are feelings about the primary reaction and include anxiety, love, contempt, pride, shame, depression.)

Strategies to Stay in Summer

It's critical to boost your family's happiness tank with activities that build bonds and strengthen your relationships. There are limitless ways to cultivate connection, but we will explore the most common and effective ways to stay in Summer.

You may read through this list and think there's no way you can stay in a sunny, positive relationship with your kids by doing these things. I admit there is nothing magical about this list.

Do you know what makes these ideas so powerful?

We *can* do them.

Do you know what makes these ideas lose all their power?

We don't do them.

The sections below are provided to give you the foundation to create lasting change in your relationship. Read through them and select one strategy you can implement today, one you can implement tomorrow, and one more you can implement by the end of this week. You will find that when you start to shift, your whole family will shift in response and you will stay in Summer longer and you will be making a happy home your top priority.

Maintain Stability

One commitment many families make to stay in Summer is to cultivate stability. Stability is any structure or system that supports healthy personal development.

Some of these structures and systems include:

- Meeting their basic needs for food, shelter, medical care
- Being loving to each other unconditionally
- Having the most regular and predictable schedule you can
- Creating a homework space with school supplies available
- Having consistent expectations for chores/responsibilities
- Having predetermined consequences for broken rules
- Living within your financial means

- Developing healthy coping strategies for stress, anger, anxiety

Stability is important for everyone, but it's essential for the health and well-being of children. When children live in a stable environment, they attend more school, earn higher grades, develop closer friendships, have better relationships with their teachers, coaches, and other adults in authority, have better eating habits, stronger hygiene habits, and possess more self-control.[17]

Two Ears, One Mouth (and Sometimes a Thing)

Happy families who stay in Summer longer know that differences or disagreements happen.

With the *Two Ears, One Mouth* strategy, you can teach your children to listen twice as much as they speak. Your child will grow more confident in sharing her feelings when she knows her family really listens to her.

If you have young children, more than two children, or very tactile children (they learn through touch) it may be difficult for them to practice the *Two Ears, One Mouth* strategy because they're bubbling with excitement. They can't help but blurt out all their thoughts!

In this case, try a physical item as a visual cue—like a talking stick—to allow the holder exclusive speaking rights. All others must wait.

Stephania struggled with empowering her daughter to share her feelings until her family implemented a special talking charm.

"Our family loves to spend time at the lake, but all of a sudden, seven-year-old Kinsey resisted when we were trying to leave. In the commotion of herding our two girls out the door, Kinsey would blurt out that she can't find her swimsuit or she doesn't have a towel or she needs a snack. I jumped in to fix everything because I just wanted to go. I asked her what the real problem was, but I didn't really listen, and we fell into Winter.

Then Leanne mentioned this strategy and I came up with a Talking Seashell (because… my girls!) and when Kinsey held it, twirling it in her hands, she told me the other day her teacher read a book about an angry crab. Then her best friend shared she saw lots of angry crabs at that same lake in some other kid's bucket. It was the first time Kinsey realized creatures lived in that water and she was now terrified of the lake. In my rush, I didn't stop and listen when she was resisting over and over, I just pushed harder. Having the *Two Ears, One Mouth* strategy meant we heard her, understood her, and were able to come up with ideas like water shoes and a floating mattress to help her feel better when we went to play."

~ *Stephania, mom of two*

Sometimes it's hard to know in the chaos of the moment if your child really needs to share something important . . . or there is something else going on. At these times, offer them your family's designated rock, stick, or seashell to signal to them they are free to speak.

More importantly, you are open to listen.

Choose the Loving Path

How would you stay in Summer in the following scenario?

Your son is about to perform his first violin solo at his school concert. Over the past week, you reminded him to play every day but two days ago he yelled at you to leave him alone. The auditorium is packed. He stands up, his shirt is wrinkly and untucked. He squeaks his first few notes and stops. Why didn't you get him to practice more? Everyone feels bad for him. He starts again and he plays the song better with just a couple of wrong notes and squeaks. You're still distracted by his shirt, but you zone back in when you hear people clapping. You join them, and he sits down and stares at the floor.

Afterwards, he looks at you and waits for your opinion.

What do you say?

Mindy (who had this experience with her son Darius) answers:

> "Our relationship had just arrived in Summer after a long Spring, so I made the conscious choice to celebrate his bravery and success. I could've come down on him in a snarky way like *that wouldn't*

> *have happened if you practiced more* or *what's going on with that shirt?* and in that second I may have felt better. But it would have destroyed any chance that we would end the conversation and still be in Summer.
>
> That night, I told him that he handled the song well, he was smart to start again, and his playing evoked emotion from the audience and they clapped really hard for his efforts.
>
> There would be other times to set a practice schedule and talk about professional appearances at concerts, but that night we stayed in Summer and we enjoyed a whole night talking like we hadn't in a while. It was heaven!"
>
> ***~ Mindy, mom of Darius***

There are countless ways that you can keep your relationship in Summer, but here are a few more ideas that might fit your family.

Scatter Your Love

Take a few moments to write an encouraging little note or draw a picture to hide for your children to find when you aren't nearby. Place it on their bathroom mirror, in their lunchbox, or in their sock drawer. A little love can go a long way! When they see your note, they will know you're thinking of them even when they aren't with you. I try to spontaneously send my teenagers funny memes or pictures so they feel a burst of love in their day.

Catch Them Doing Good

Notice your kids when they do something caring, generous, or kind. Tell them with specific words (not empty praise) that you appreciate their effort. Their actions can be as simple as putting their toys/dishes/laundry away, picking up something that was left on the floor/counter/sofa, or sharing their toys/snacks/space with someone else. What we focus on grows—so focusing on good leads to more good behavior.

Find Activities for Everyone

Don't underestimate the power of connection during a good family game.

Kids love to understand and operate inside a set of rules that are the same for everyone. There's nothing better than seeing your child work her way through a game, winning some, losing some, and sometimes becoming the family champion for the week.

> "We go through phases where we play cards every few nights for a month, and then I'll set up a puzzle and we all gather and work on it spontaneously. We might pull out old school games like Life or Clue, and then newer games like Apples to Apples. Now that my kids are getting older, they're asking us to play their games. They feel very proud to teach us the strategy and often beat us!"
>
> ~ ***Bettina, mom of two***

Physically Connect

Families who stay in Summer find ways to be physically close to each other. Whether the child's love language is physical touch or not, we crave human touch. Yes, even teens!

As a young child, it's easy to tickle and wrestle and play on the floor, but as your child gets older, you'll need to find new ways to stay in touch. If your child enjoys a massage to their shoulders, hands, or feet, use it as an opportunity for them to open up because they feel emotionally safe to connect.

Other examples include brushing their hair, giving them a new hairstyle, lying side by side while reading, snuggling under a blanket during a movie, or having a secret handshake.

Relive the Good Old Days

When everyone is firmly planted in Summer and the connection between your family is strong, show them their first baby clothes, your report card from middle school, or photos of your family when they were little.

When they feel like an integral part of a family unit, or a larger tribe, they make connections to more of the world around them. As an ongoing commitment to celebrating your family, share recent memories with ticket stubs, park passes, or photos.

I set aside time after a vacation to create a slide-show of our favorite moments. After we've been home for a week or two, we gather together and relive the happy moments, sharing stories, and deepening the memories of the fun times. It helps give us common memories to relive—even months later.

Find a Cause

A powerful connection exercise is working together to support people in need. There's a huge market for voluntourism—where families can dig wells in Tanzania or build a school in Peru . . . but there are countless opportunities in your own town that can fit your family perfectly. Many non-profit organizations operate solely on the generosity of volunteers. They accept help in many ways.

"Volunteering as a family gets people back out in the community, and the whole experience gives kids greater self-esteem," says Heather Jack, founder of *The Volunteer Family*. "According to a study by The Search Institute, young people are 50 percent less likely to abuse drugs, alcohol, cigarettes, or engage in other destructive behavior if they volunteer at least one hour per week," Jack says. When children watch their parents give to others, they begin to understand what it takes to be committed to something worthwhile.[18]

If your family is new to volunteering, consider activities like:

- participating in a 1K or 5K fundraising walk
- visiting a nursing home to talk or read with residents
- sorting bags of food at a food pantry
- donating blankets and tennis balls to an animal shelter
- collecting cloths or school supplies for foster children
- participating in public space or beach clean-up days
- sending care boxes to troops overseas
- shopping for a family who is busy with a sick child

> "One annual fundraising event that my family does together is the 5K Winter Pineapple Classic that benefits the Leukemia and Lymphoma Society. We started running this after I was diagnosed with a chronic form of Leukemia (CLL) when my kids were 5 and 7, and they contribute by running the race and raising funds. We love doing this fundraiser together —we get dirty, wet, sudsy, cold, and tired. Every year we create memories that will last a lifetime."
>
> ***~Julie, mom of two***

The sweetness of summer is intoxicating! We want the happiness, joy, gratitude, love, and true connection with our children to last forever.

When I reflect on my family's best Summer days, I see that we are a source of joy and happiness for each other. We offer a place to learn compassion, generosity, and service. We nurture an environment to support all our hopes, dreams, and aspirations. And we provide a cradle of safety in times of chaos or confusion.

The 5 Seasons of Connection was created to check in with ourselves and our relationships with our kids. It keeps us in a state of mutual respect, happiness, and collaboration. I want to live in an enduring state of Summer with my children and I know you want that too.

And, life happens.

As much as we want to stay in Summer, inevitably a thick cloud moves in front of the sun, dark shadows fill the sky, and the breeze shifts to a chilly blast.

That, dear parents, is the season of Fall creeping into our lives.

We have to take swift and decisive action to pull our family back from the brink of disconnection. If we can't/won't/don't, an unwelcomed chill in the air signals our relationships are moving into the next season.

Summertime is always the best of what might be.

~ Charles Bowden, Author and Journalist

CHAPTER 5

Fall

....

F*all is a period* of time when the earth tilts away from the sun, resulting in less daylight, cooling temperatures, and dropping leaves—not all at once. Slowly. One day you look around and all the leaves are gone!

Similarly, in *The 5 Seasons of Connection*, Fall creeps in. When we finally feel the chill, we stop and wonder. *Hold on. Where did all the fun, happy times go? It was so great and now they're gone.*

Children can take us to our edge. They might poke and press and test and try to get their way. They throw sass around like confetti. They roll their eyes. They ignore, deny, or defy. They huff and puff and try to blow our happy house down.

Yet, none of these behaviors are Fall.

What is Fall?

Fall happens when *both sides* of the relationship pull back from connection.

The start of this season looks different for every family, but everyone can remember instances when they noticed it.

Here are just a few:

- Your son was worried about his science test. When he gets home you ask, "Hey sweetie! How was your test?" He's caught off guard and snaps, "Stop pressuring me!"
- Your son is at his friend's house starving and he texts you asking if you could make dinner. You joyfully prepare it and text him back it's ready. He doesn't respond so you text him again. Then he sends you a picture of them eating burgers in the backyard and a note he'll be home by 10pm.
- Your daughter asks to go to the mall with her friends. You agree as long as she empties the trash first. You come home with groceries and notice it wasn't done. When she walks in, you say, "You didn't empty the garbage before you left." She replies, "Chill out. I'll do it now, it's no big deal."

Some would say it's inevitable that our kids initiate the onset of Fall because of the ways they test our limits, but they don't bring us into Fall alone. It's the fiery combination of their action and *our* reaction. We don't just *fall* into Fall—we get here because the bountiful Summer garden was neglected and weeds are choking the once-abundant growth.

When life gets busy or chaotic, we may neglect our relationship with our kids, leaving it vulnerable to the onset of Fall.

When our relationship heads towards Fall, we feel:

- Caught off guard by something sharp your child says.
- A lack of playful, light feelings in your interactions.

- Physically and emotionally distant from your kids.
- No chit chat, just talking to share necessary info.
- Impatience around their perceived shortcomings.
- A new chill in the air.

When you're heading towards Fall, your child feels:

- A need to pull back from spending time with you.
- Obliged to only give short, pointed answers.
- Impatient, huffing, puffing, eye rolling.
- Uninterested in small talk or stories.
- Closed body language, looking down, looking away.
- Emotionally hiding behind devices when you're near.
- Physically hibernating by being alone in their room.
- Resistant to chores.

Why Our Children Go to Fall

Our kids often slip towards Fall for three main reasons: they feel a lack of control, they have unmet needs, or their expectations don't match reality.

Most children don't manage their time, obligations, daily schedule, activities, or food choices. They need to maneuver through lots of transitions each day, which can keep them feeling unsettled. If they perceive this unsettled feeling to be a threat, they almost always choose fight over flight. They want to take control of something and they want to stay connected to you.

I can hear you now... what?

If my child wants to connect with me, why not ask me about *my* day? Why would she push *my* buttons?

Children are like flood waters draining to a river—they take the path of least resistance. Kids are little people, but they aren't little *adults*. Even your 14-year-old son, who is 165 pounds and 6-foot-tall, isn't a little adult. Their brains still resort to young-child strategies of *any attention is good attention*. Our children work tirelessly to successfully engage us—and that engagement can be positive or negative.

If there's too much negative pressure on your relationship, you may descend into dark, stormy times. But Fall doesn't have to be the last stop before a certain Winter. Use it as an indicator that things are changing, and our attention is required.

Just like the weeds that popped up in our beautiful Summer garden threaten to damage our harvest, neglecting key practices will damage your resilience and resolve as a parent.

Back Talking, Sassy, Snarky Responses

You may call back talking different things, but chances are you know exactly what it is.

If you're like most parents, it pushes a hot button deep in your soul. Back talk is most often your child's way of expressing anger, fear, frustration, or hurt and they don't have the skills or tools to express it any other way.

It's easy for parents to feel slighted or hurt when their child acts sassy or snarky but trust me—sassing is not a battle you need to dive into with your child for a few reasons.

One, when they use sassy or snarky language, they're practicing in their safe space for the times they'll use it in situations with peer pressure.

Two, it isn't about the sass. It's a power struggle to deflect from a deeper issue. That is where you need to focus your attention. Are they coming to the interaction feeling hurt, rejected, embarrassed, or vulnerable? The bad attitude is designed to hide their true feelings.

Your child is trying to connect with you using the tool that's easiest to access in their toolbox. If you jump straight to disciplining him for his snarkiness, he may think you don't understand his underlying feelings. He'll most likely ramp up his reaction to show you just how upset he is.

Instead of talking about the sass, acknowledge his emotions. For example, you can say, "Wow, you sound really frustrated about what happened." Put the focus on the feeling. Extend your hand and bring her close to you. Tell her you love her. Sprinkle her with gratitude and appreciation. You can do this much easier when you're in a good place in your own personal season.

So, let's check in. Are you coming to this interaction with your child from a place of your personal Summer?

Or are you already in Fall?

Quick Life Check-Up

Without question, you can't be who your child needs when you come to the interaction feeling stretched, stressed, or depleted. This quick check-up is a snapshot of where you are right now, evaluating if you're ready to engage or if you need to take time to get centered because you are being pulled in too many directions.

Answer yes or no to the following questions:

Feelings Assessment

Y	N	Do you think about all the ways you aren't appreciated?
Y	N	Do you take your child's slight as defiance or a dismissal?
Y	N	Is hurt or resentment building inside of you?
Y	N	Are you collecting evidence that you've been disrespected?
Y	N	Do you fill in the gaps with things implied or assumed?
Y	N	Are you holding back from giving and receiving love freely?
Y	N	Are you so fixed on one outcome that all changes disrupt?
Y	N	Do you feel like the grass is greener elsewhere?

Physical Assessment

Y	N	Are you responding more with sarcasm or snarkiness?
Y	N	Is your voice saying one thing and your body saying another?
Y	N	Are your shoulders tight, breathing shallow, jaw clenched?
Y	N	Are you hungry? Thirsty? Tired? Sick?

Y	N	Are you cutting out time to exercise your body?
Y	N	Are you pushing yourself without restful/restorative sleep?
Y	N	Have you felt stress in your belly or through headaches?
Y	N	Have you deprioritized fresh air and outdoor activities?

Emotional Assessment

Y	N	Have you neglected your self-care practices?
Y	N	Have you avoided journal writing to express yourself?
Y	N	Are you surrounded by clutter or chaos?
Y	N	Have you cancelled plans to connect with friends?
Y	N	Have you turned to destructive habits to get through?
Y	N	Are you zoning out on TV or social media?
Y	N	Have you said 'yes' to too many commitments?
Y	N	Are you giving with an expectation of receiving?

If you answered *yes* to:

5 or less: You may need a little support to get back to Summer.

6 or more: You are at risk of entering Fall, or you're there now.

10 or more: You are heading towards Winter.

Your ability to regulate your reactions is predicated on your current level of self-care. If you haven't been regularly investing in your spiritual, emotional, physical, relational, intellectual, or occupational well-being, you're less equipped to bring your child back to Summer.

Once you know where you are, we need to explore our children's role in bringing us to Fall's doorstep. Remembering their natural tendencies—as well as monitoring their behaviors for consistent and predictable patterns that trigger chilly temperatures—is one way to do that.

What You Know

If your children need more time to process information, or more time to transition, or if on their journey from A-Z they zigzag to visit F, Q, and T first, build that into your day. With a buffer, you won't accidentally push your relationship deeper into Fall by running on your timetable and neglecting your child's natural tendencies to meander.

Your frustration is your responsibility. You need to recognize your child's temperament as a valid consideration in your planning. Perhaps you've noticed that your child struggles more at certain times or on certain days. Recognizing that pattern will help you find your way out of Fall.

Personal Rhythms

We often don't think about our child's personal rhythms in Summer because the flow is smooth and easy. When Fall's chill hits the air, it's time to focus on the ups and downs of their energy, attention, and level of cooperation. See where they lose control and open the door for Fall.

Is it after school on Mondays? Fridays?

Before gymnastics class or baseball?

During dinner or math homework?

After playing his favorite video game?

After coming home from a friend's house?

Is it during your family's witching hour—the daily period of high stress—either early morning, the hour before dinner, bedtime—maybe all three?

In that moment when your child's behavior brings Fall back, remember they're feeling something: misunderstood, unloved, afraid, or neglected. We can't build contingencies against all the challenges in their lives every day, but the magic of knowing their personal rhythms gives you the opportunity to guide them back toward Summer. They feel the feeling, understand it, and release it.

Fall often creeps into our lives like dandelions. If we look at our current distractions, we can see how we missed the weeds that popped up. What demanded our attention? What were we consumed with recently? Were our children feeling loved, honored, cherished, and heard, or were they competing with our giant to-do list?

One way we often slip into Fall is by allocating our time in ways that lead us toward disconnection. Too many activities or obligations pull us apart emotionally or physically.

Important vs. Not Important

Why does this matter when you are faced with Fall?

In the rush of life, it's easy to jump into reaction mode. We scramble to take on every single thing as they pop up. We focus intently on that until the next thing pops up. The feeling that you have lost control can trigger you in times of opposition. Your child will be lost in the whirlwind of unfinished tasks and unfulfilled promises. If you're stretched thin across things that don't matter, your child isn't going to get the best version of you.

What do you have on your list that is *truly* important?

What needs to be done today? This week? This month?

If you're like me, your list gets filled with (some) important and (too many) unimportant tasks. When we're pulled in too many directions or juggling too many things, we put ourselves in the path of the perfect storm: disconnection, defensive or harsh responses, all-or-nothing thinking, or blaming/shaming cycles blow in.

What Have You Been Prioritizing Lately?

Take a look at your calendar or your to-do list. What is taking up the most time? Are there things that you could:

- Accelerate? (Cut the dilly-dallying and get it done.)
- Automate? (Set up bill payments/order more online)
- Consolidate? (Do it with something/someone else.)
- Eliminate? (Delegate or decide it isn't important.)

Spend a few moments and go through your calendar and to-do list with the courage to remove all unnecessary tasks. Now that we've streamlined and decluttered our week, let's intentionally prioritize the people and commitments we value the most.

- Do you have activities that connects and impacts everyone, like shared games, hobbies, or sports?
- Do you have time blocked off for some self-care?
- How many opportunities do you have to spend quality time with your children 1:1?

We want to leave Fall and head back to the beautiful, connected days of Summer, but dreaming isn't doing. If we say our children are our highest priority, we need to reflect that in how we spend our time.

When Fall comes in real life, the leaves change color and the temperature drops. In *The 5 Seasons of Connection*, Fall is less tactile. Our relationship changes when we feel distance growing between us and chilliness in our interactions. Fall can creep into your family because you snapped, your child dissed you, or life pulled you too thin.

It can (and does!) happen to us at any time, but it's important to catch it early, identify what caused Fall to arrive this time, decide to build new habits to prevent it from happening again, and bring your family back to Summer, where you feel connected, warm, open, and receptive.

What happens when you're struggling in Fall, wanting to go

back to Summer, but anxious that you're headed towards Winter?

You, my friend, have arrived at the Crossroads, our 5th season.

CHAPTER 6

Crossroads

• • • • • • •

This is the season we have been waiting for!

We started with the cold, disconnected season of Winter, where parents and kids weren't working as a team but in opposition.

We moved to the Spring thaw and explored an extensive list of opportunities for connection. We learned how to reestablish good relations and bring back a few more smiles, a few more conversations, and a few more moments of togetherness.

After planting the seeds in Spring, we fully enjoyed Summer, the sweetest season full of growth, blossoms, beauty, joy, fullness, warmth, and the fruits of our labor. Our families thrive in Summer while sharing and caring, conversing and connecting.

In Fall, we noticed that we weren't really paying close attention to our garden and it suffered a bit from neglect. Weeds and critters popped up, threatening our harvest. It's when we think everything is going great that we stop noticing the small signs, the little inconsistencies in their behavior. We don't see that our connection is slipping and we find ourselves in Fall.

We can get back to Summer with dedication and intentional

work, but it won't happen because you wish it to, want it to, or force it to.

You're now so curious about what comes next, I know!

The 5th season is where you hold the ultimate influence over how your interaction will end. The 5th season is where the power lies. It is choice. It is possibility.

It is the Crossroads.

What is the Crossroads?

When our relationship is at the Crossroads, we may feel:

- Torn between reacting (which moves us towards Winter) and responding (which moves us towards Summer).
- Anxious about which path to take out of an interaction.
- Emotional, triggered, withdrawn and hesitant, all at once.
- Impatient to get through the interaction or solve the issue.
- Intent to gather all necessary info to make a solid choice.

When our relationship is at the Crossroads, our child may feel:

- Unsettled about what to do/what to expect next.
- Eager to force a decision.
- A little scattered or rattled emotionally.
- Afraid of the pause before a decision, reaction, or response.

The 5th season is the most visited season of all. You could face the Crossroads ten, twenty, thirty times a day with your children. You could swing from Summer to Fall to Summer to Fall to Winter to Spring to Summer in an afternoon and between every shift you'll come to the Crossroads. So, in other words, every single time you interact with your child and you face two or more ways to respond or react to handle a situation, you're at the Crossroads.

Every interaction is a choice.

If they snap at us, do we bark back? Or do we ask open ended questions and draw out more information? When they respond with sassy or snarky answers, do we request kindness? Or do we respond with our own sharp attitude?

The Crossroads is the moment we pause, first to reflect, then to respond, reducing the force and intensity of our reactions.

The Pause

Why is there so much power in the pause?

First and foremost, it gives us time to assess where we are in the moment. Are we coming from a place of fullness or depletion? What hot button was pushed? What trigger was activated?

Once we have checked ourselves, we can assess our child. Is there a stressor we can easily see (exhaustion, hunger, failed test, not making the sports team) or a stressor we can't easily see (broken friendship, worry, stress, feelings of rejection, hormones, fear of failure, embarrassment)?

Second, the pause gives us the opportunity to choose how we'll handle it.

Maybe it's an opportunity to step away from your child so she can reflect on her behavior. Maybe it's an opportunity to lean in, gently asking questions to help him refocus on how his behavior makes him feel and how it impacts others.

Or maybe it's an opportunity to sit silently and hold space for her to find her center.

Let's explore that more.

Holding Space

What is holding space?

Holding space means we are willing to be beside another person on her journey without judging her, trying to fix her, bring up any inadequacies or problems in her ideas, or trying to impact the outcome of her choices.

When we *hold space* for other people, we truly open our hearts. We offer unconditional support and let go of judgment and control. *Holding space* is sitting patiently at the Crossroads without being invested in a specific outcome, even if you have ideas or solutions.

Opposing Feelings

The internal conflict you will feel at the Crossroads is a true struggle because it involves two opposing feelings.

Now, you are looking down both paths.

On the one hand, you may be very angry, disappointed, hurt, or frustrated with your child. Their behavior may have triggered some fear or touched on a hot button issue. On the other hand, you may want to help them, take over for them, protect them, or roll back time to before they made the decision that brought you to the Crossroads. Both feelings are valid and real.

If you berate, lash out, yell, ridicule, shame, mock, judge, or insult, you will absolutely find yourself in Winter.

If you inquire, support, validate, empathize, or simply listen, you will most likely end up in Spring, maybe even Summer. This doesn't mean that you won't feel angry, hurt, or disappointed; it just means that you're choosing not to act out your feelings in a negative way.

The First of Many

You will face many situations for the first time on your parenting journey. The first time your child hits someone at preschool. The first time your child is bullied at the park. The first time he steals or swears or screams, "I hate you." There will be no shortage of opportunities for you to stand at the Crossroads.

Even if you haven't had direct experience with a *first time* issue, you have faced other situations where you stood at the Crossroads and had to choose between two options. Pull those past experiences to assist with future events.

When your child unleashes a storm, the most likely reaction is to match the rising energy with your own fiery emotions. Science backs this up: Newton's third law states that for every action there is an equal and opposite reaction. However, Newton didn't take into account the power of choice to override our long-held beliefs or patterns. We can stand at the Crossroads and choose to return to Summer. I'm going to be honest, this takes time, practice, and deliberate concentration and intention.

Despite the release of adrenalin and the flooding of fight or flight responses, you can use calming techniques. Practice deep breathing and respond as if you were talking to a respected elder and not your out-of-control child.

This is not to say that you should deny your feelings and suppress your reaction.

We are humans living a human experience. However, there's a difference between how you *feel* and how you *express*. At the Crossroads of an interaction, you'll need to build a bridge of connectiveness with your child and put aside feelings of punishment, retaliation, rage, hurt, disappointment, or worry in order to stay in Summer. Focus on feelings that come from a place of warmth, guidance, teaching, education, and partnership.

The Crossroads is there when you're faced with a decision in the moment, but it also allows you to evaluate your current path and decide if it still fits your family.

There have been times when parents headed down one path and noticed that pressure and stress had started to build. So they created a Crossroads right there to check in and see if they were aligned or if they needed to course correct.

Course Corrections

Erin typically resisted change, but when she finally course corrected her kids' activities, it made all the difference for them.

> "My twin boys were competitive swimmers and we did all the early morning practices and late-night meets. James was totally into it but Julian started to dislike it more and more.
>
> After a big competition, Julian blurted out

that he wanted to quit and try martial arts. My old, knee-jerk reaction would have been to snap back and say "No! Quitting will make our schedule too hard," or "James hit a low point but kept going, you can too." I had recently learned about *The 5 Seasons of Connection* and realized I was at the Crossroads.

Do I let him quit and support his interest to try martial arts? Or do I dig in my heels and insist he continue competing even if he is miserable? When I looked down both paths, I wasn't honoring Julian by locking him into an activity he didn't want to do. We found a studio near our house that he could bike to so we all felt it was a win. Now both boys are flourishing, our family went back into Summer. Understanding the Crossroads made all the difference for us."

~ Erin, mom of twin boys

You've Been at the Crossroads Before

Think back to another time in your life when you felt angry, hurt, or disappointed. How did you come through that experience?

Did you journal?

Did you talk it out with a loved one?

Did you choose to focus on the positivity in your life?

Did you recommit to your desired outcome and move past it?

Even though it's hard, and being at the Crossroads feels

uncomfortable or stressful, we're very blessed to have a lifetime of experiences to use as inspiration. On top of using our past experiences to guide us along our parenting journey, we can also use our time at the Crossroads to tap into our 6th sense.

Our intuition.

Intuition

Intuition is the ability to understand something without any evidence or conscious reasoning. It can play a critical role in our lives if we allow it.

We can feel our intuition kick into overdrive many times on the parenting journey from the time when our kids are being too quiet, to the time that our teens start hiding things from us. Somehow we just know there is more! Being still and listening to that inner voice can guide you through a particularly tough Crossroads.

> *The intuitive mind is a sacred gift and the rational mind is a faithful servant. We have created a society that honors the servant and has forgotten the gift.*
>
> ***~ Albert Einstein, Theoretical Physicist and Author***

Recently, Mai-lin's relationship with her daughter was strained.

Over the past few weeks, Sophie came home from dance practice or piano class and went straight to her room. One night, Mai-lin went into Sophie's room to talk. As usual her daughter asked her to leave. Mai-lin said she knew something was wrong and resisted leaving, but Sophie snapped and yelled at her to get out.

Mai-lin left but knew intuitively something wasn't right.

Well past midnight, Mai-lin couldn't shake her feeling. She went in to sit beside her daughter's bed. In the darkness, Sophie's phone lit up with a text message. Mai-lin opened it and lost her breath.

Nearly thirty text messages filled with foul language, threats, and promises of violence were on her phone. Mai-lin was so grateful she had trusted her instinct, but her heart broke.

> "When I stood at the Crossroads, I looked both ways.
>
> Down one path was my current life with my silently suffering daughter pushing me away. It felt like Winter for me because I was completely shut out. Down the other path, the path where I expose her abusers, I could see Sophie being very angry and embarrassed and terrified, but hopefully safe. That felt like less of a Winter.
>
> I talked to her in the morning. At first she tried to hide it, but I was soft and gentle, so loving, so compassionate. I came from my best Summer self. Very soon she broke down and asked me to make them stop. I turned to the school and the police. Thankfully, it ended. We didn't end up in Winter at all. I'm so grateful I trusted my gut."
>
> ~ ***Mai-lin, mom of Sophie***

As parents, I believe we are energetically and spiritually connected to our children. But our logical, rational side often overpowers our 6th sense. We second-guess ourselves, or even worse, mock ourselves for having an active imagination. Our intuition isn't a magic power that will lead us astray. It's actually our brain's true super power. It collects, categorizes, and synthesizes thousands of pieces of information that swirl around us, whether we are conscious of it or not, and our brain reveals a full picture created from our patterns and our experiences in the form of intuition or gut instincts.

To tap into our deeper reserves of our brain's capabilities and make well-informed, well-supported decisions about our child's well-being, safety or security, we need to quiet our inner noise, go to a place of inner peace, and explore all our thoughts and feelings without filtering them through our mind's logical, rational, evidence-based filter. When we stand at the Crossroads, we can build or burn a bridge, but only one of them brings you to deeper connection with your children.

This 5th season is the pinnacle of parenting. Once we master it, we can guide our relationships and family communication much more smoothly. We can skillfully read the weather in our interactions and know if pressure is building, or if sunny skies are ahead. Sometimes we might be blessed with art in the sky.

Watch for Rainbows

A rainbow is an arc of color that appears when millions of water droplets reflect and refract sunlight in the sky.

Historically and symbolically, rainbows have held a mystical role in our culture. The fact that these beautiful and awe-inspiring gifts from nature often follow the harshest, darkest storms has led us to believe that rainbows are the promise of hope and the presence of blessings. We can't touch them, feel them, or save them for later, but when they light up in sky, we stop to appreciate their beauty. Here is another chance for us to pause.

In your relationship with your child, a rainbow could appear unexpectedly in the middle of an interaction and it's something we might miss if our heads were down or our focus spotlighting on a small portion of the scene. When we are pausing at the Crossroads, we can breathe, listen, think, and notice these gifts and often we come up with our best outcome. Sometimes the rainbow acts as the bridge to take you from one season to another.

What does a rainbow in your relationship look like?

Maybe your child comes home after visiting friends and surprises you with an apology for purposely pushing your hot button earlier. Perhaps you're driving your son to practice and a song comes on and you look at each other, smile, and sing.

These rainbow moments are fleeting and easy to miss if you manage your emotions by being busy or stay so focused on your anger that you can't see the opportunity to move towards Summer with your child.

Now that we understand the powers of all the seasons—and how to navigate them individually—let's discover how deeply they impact our lives. In Part 2, we will learn more about ourselves, our values, our aspirations, and our hopes for our families.

When you have once seen
the glow of happiness on the face of a beloved person,
you know that a man can have no vocation
but to awaken that light on the faces surrounding him.
In the depth of winter, I finally learned that within me
there lay an invincible summer.

~ Albert Camus,
Philosopher and Author

CHAPTER 7

The Five Elements of Awareness

•••••••

There are five elements that every family needs as the foundation for open communication and loving connection.

When we have these five elements in place, we enjoy several benefits such as:

- Greater understanding
- More compassion
- Collaborative problem-solving efforts
- Stronger family bonds

These benefits support each family member during the ups and downs—or Summers and Winters—of life.

Typically, when our children are very little, it's a one-way street. They signal to us that they have an unmet need and we vigorously try to meet those needs.

Then they grow a bit. Their needs change. They start voicing their opinions, begin advocating for how they want things done, and make decisions to benefit themselves without considering the bigger picture. This is when the relationship enters a two-way phase.

In the two-way phase, our children will continue to have needs they want met. We will start to have needs we want met, which may or may not occur. (Think about the ongoing challenges your family might face at bedtime, mealtime, bath time, or even getting out of the house in the morning). When our relationship enters this stage, there will be ample opportunities for resistance or conflicts. It signals that it's time to lay the foundation with the Five Elements of Awareness.

Understanding these five elements allows us to navigate our way through the various seasons toward Summer with our kids. They are:

1. Personal Core Values
2. Family Values
3. Goals and Priorities
4. Temperament
5. Communication Style

The more you know about these five foundational elements, the easier it is to be the parent you want to be. Of course, you can always descend into disconnection because one of you is exhausted, hungry, hurt, rejected, or feeling out of control. But if you truly know yourself and your child, you can take inspired action to lessen the impact of these external variables.

Where Does Happiness Come From?

Some people think they have little control over their lives or their children, but that isn't what the science shows.

Happiness expert Sonja Lyubomirsky, Ph.D. is a professor in the Department of Psychology at the University of California, Riverside and author of the bestseller *The How of Happiness: A Scientific Approach to Getting the Life You Want*, a how-to book to increase your happiness-based on science[19].

Dr. Lyubomirsky shares that when studying happiness, she found that 40% of our happiness comes from what we do and how we think, 10% comes from external factors (finances, career, health, climate, etc.), and 50% comes from our genetically predetermined natural temperament.

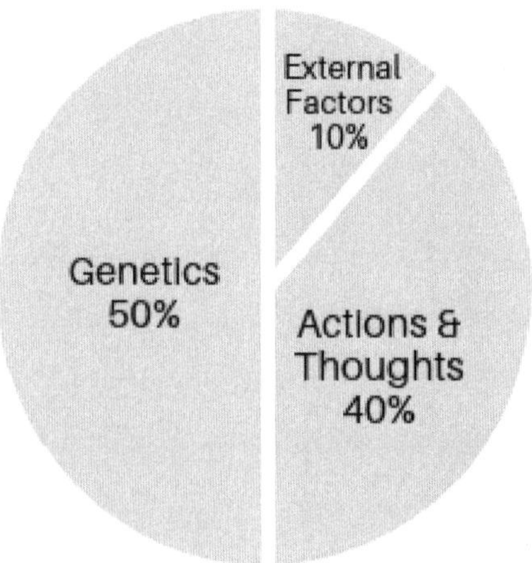

Source: Sonja Lyubomirsky, Ph.D., University of California, Riverside

According to Dr. Lyubomirsky, we can control 40% of our happiness-potential simply by being and doing.

To be fair, we don't purposefully decide on every thought as it enters our mind. In fact, we have a deep reservoir of subconscious and unconscious beliefs that filter many of our experiences for us. As parents—and as people—we have a set of core values and beliefs that invisibly shape how we see the world and what we believe to be true, impacting how we make decisions and how we navigate our lives.

If we aren't aware of these thoughts, where do they come from? It's time to identify and honor our Core Values.

CHAPTER 8:

Element One: Personal Core Values

•••••••

The first step comes from advice given over a thousand years ago:

Know thyself.

written on the temple of the oracle in Delphi

What is a Core Value? And why does it help to know yourself?

Whether you're aware of it or not, your Core Values are the pulse and power beneath all your decisions. They are the rules that guide you through life's ups and downs. They determine your answers to questions like *who am I?* and *what do I stand for?* Core Values help you set priorities. They are the fundamental forces that drive your decisions.

Let's test it.

Decide if you agree or disagree with the following statements:

- It's fine to go to bed without brushing your teeth.
- My toddler uses his iPad daily so he'll be tech-savvy.

- It's not natural for boys to cry. He needs to be a man.
- I pay my kids for chores to learn the value of a dollar.
- My child eats the same food as us or he can go hungry.

Whether you agree or disagree with these statements is based solely on your personal Core Value system.

Look at the list again.

Do you know someone who would select an answer different than your response? You very well might! Whether it's someone else in your family, at your work, or in your community, you likely know someone who is similar to you in many ways. Then *boom*—you fall into an argument over politics, religion, ethics, economics, or culture. In that heated conversation, you just can't believe he thinks that way on the topic.

Chances are, you were having a values conflict. Different things matter to each of you.

When you start listening to conversations around you, it becomes easier to identify people's deeply-rooted belief systems as they go about their daily lives.

While at the gym one week, I noticed a conversation between two women quickly heat up when a newscaster mentioned a celebrity was launching a glamour make-up kit for little girls. Two sets of images of girls ages five to nine popped up. The first set showed them natural and child-like. The second set showed them with multiple shades of glittering eye shadow, mascara on their lashes, contour and shimmer highlights expertly applied to their cheeks, and various shades of pink on their lips.

Their conversation went like this:

> First lady: Look at those little angels! They're so beautiful. Look how their eyes just pop. That one got her freckles covered up. She looks so flawless now!
>
> Second lady: I can't believe someone would take those innocent children and slather them with all that crap! Hiding freckles? They don't need to be hidden. Do we need to teach these girls that every difference and deviation from some fake ideal is what they should strive for?
>
> First lady: What do you mean? They look great! They need to put their best foot forward and they're learning how to do that early. What if she didn't like her freckles? Should she have to see them every day?
>
> Second lady: They look like miniature women. These girls are beautiful just the way they are. Now they're going to think they need this garbage on their faces. Childhood innocence set on fire right there, I say.

> First lady: You're overreacting. It's not like they are going to do all this for school. But it's great for special occasions.
>
> Second lady: When you first started wearing makeup, or coloring your hair, or shaving your legs, did you do it once for a special occasion and never again? No. Of course not. You felt the need to keep doing it. This is just terrible.
>
> First lady: Well, I think they look gorgeous! I might order a kit for my daughter. How fun to do our makeup together!

You might feel like you align with the first lady, the second, or somewhere in between. Either way, the feelings you have about glamour make-up on little girls is based exclusively on your Core Value system, just like every other stand you take on issues.

Knowing your Core Values gives you a clear and solid framework to make better decisions for yourself, and because you are a parent, make better decisions for your family.

The Origin

Where do these values come from?

Your values have been passed down through generations. They combine the experience of your life, your parent's lives, and their parents before them. Some of these are rooted in culture, religion, or politics. Some are based in privilege, hardships, or survival.

Wherever they come from, they're the beliefs that form our worldview or philosophical perspective. They define us. They become the values that we fight for in areas of justice, equality, or human rights when we feel threatened. These Core Values also influence what we believe *and* what we are willing to believe, which comes into play every day as parents.

Let's look at one common parenting scenario—a child not telling the truth.

If truthfulness isn't one of your top five Personal Core Values and your child lies, you will likely tell her to be honest next time and move on. You may not feel an emotional impact.

If truthfulness is one of your top five Personal Core Values and your child lies to you, it can trigger something deep within you and you could respond fiercely, surprising even yourself with your fury.

Here's an example.

Farrah was a pretty relaxed and confident mom. However, one day she was completely blindsided by an intense reaction over her Core Value of honesty.

Her six-year old daughter Hannah had been asking for a retractable four-color pen. In every store they visited, Hannah begged, and Farrah repeatedly said no. A few days went by. While checking her daughter's homework, Farrah noticed words written in green, red, black, and blue ink.

"Hannah," she asked, "how did you write in these colors?"

Her child proudly pulled out the exact pen she had been

begging to have. Farrah quickly asked, "We didn't buy you that pen, honey. Where did you get it?"

Hannah effortlessly said her friend gave it to her. But then she stumbled when retelling her story. Farrah knew she was lying.

"You have one chance to tell the truth," Farrah warned her. Hannah insisted it was the truth. Farrah experienced a burning in her belly unlike anything she felt before. She erupted and yelled at the top of her lungs. Hannah started to cry. She tried to run to her room, but Farrah blocked the hall. She yelled until her throat hurt, then ordered Hannah to think about how damaging lying could be.

But Hannah could only think about her mom's terrifying rage.

Farrah went outside to calm down. Guilt and regret consumed her. It was a pen. Hannah was six years old. Her tiny, sweet child hadn't learned anything about telling the truth—she learned her mother could come totally unhinged.

Farrah went to apologize for losing her temper. Hannah jumped into her arms, squeezing her tightly.

"Ms. Tina says when we get super mad we should count to 100," Hannah said. "Let's count, mommy."

Love for her compassionate and forgiving child flooded her. Hannah brought them back to Summer with her act of love but Farrah still wanted to dig into why she erupted as ferociously as she did so she came to me for help. We worked on the Core Value exercise together and I could feel that there was more Farrah needed to uncover so I gave her some journal prompts to work on and we met again after a few weeks. She said:

"I didn't realize a few things. First, I didn't realize that I had this huge collection of invisible beliefs that were driving my life decisions, many of them planted in my subconscious from when I was younger than my six-year old daughter. I didn't realize that I could be so reactive when something outside of me clashed with something inside of me. But, the biggest a-ha was that I was parenting with a playbook that I didn't like so diving deeply into my core values helped me to name them and then actively choose the ones that I wanted to keep, and work on evolving the ones I didn't. My daughter flat-out lying was like tossing a match on a pile of dry kindling but after journaling and going deeper into my own life history, I found the root cause. My mother was a chronic liar and it caused her to be fired from many jobs, evicted from many apartments, and made our family suffer massive hardship. My parents split and I knew it was because of all the turmoil that her lying brought into our family. Eventually, I stopped seeing her because of so many reasons but I didn't consider how deeply I was wounded from her straight-faced lies until I felt the powerlessness and pent-up rage explode with Hannah. I wasn't the same person or the same parent after learning about core values,

> and then deciding to evolve from who I was to who I wanted to be.
>
> ***~ Farrah, mom of Hannah***

Over the years, I've heard from many moms who felt awful when they reacted explosively like Farrah. Most were shocked and surprised they reacted with that much rage and they became afraid of when they would erupt again.

Fortunately, after working through the Core Value exercise below, these women could predict what scenarios would likely push them over their edge. They could work proactively to prevent future eruptions and long Winter days with their kids.

For many families, though, there isn't one single value system at play because each parent brings their own history, experiences, and beliefs to the parenting journey. If your family experiences frequent or repeated misunderstandings, conflict, or arguments, it's most likely a clash of two systems.

Two Parents, Two Core Value Systems

In two-parent families, it's ideal that both parents complete their own Personal Core Value exercise. Your parenting decisions are influenced by two separate and independent sets of Core Values. We often don't know if we're aligned or misaligned until the moment our child pushes a hot button and elicits two very different reactions.

Let's see how this unfolded for this family.

Eight-year-old Will saw a plate of chocolate cookies sitting on the counter, fresh from the oven.

He asked his mom if he could have one. She said no, they were made to eat when his friends came over later that day. Will waited for her to leave the kitchen, then raced to the plate and ate a few cookies. His mother returned to the kitchen and saw him chewing.

Mom: You took the cookies after I told you no? Did you not understand what I said? I said no cookies. Now you don't get any more cookies when your friends come over today.

Dad: He's just a kid eating cookies. What's the problem?

Mom: He was told no cookies and he did it anyway. There are rules and they need to be followed.

Dad: Rules are meant to be broken, right? Come on, cut him some slack. You should be happy I didn't eat them all myself. They smell amazing. You know they're best when they're hot. Don't make him sit there and watch all his friends eat cookies and he can't. That's ridiculous.

Mom: It is not ridiculous! He knew the rule, he broke the rule, he will have the consequence of that action. There is no gray area here.

Dad: Look, he's so sad. How about no treats

> tomorrow, ok? Look, honey. No treats tomorrow.
>
> Mom: You are totally undermining me. Now if I make him follow the rules, I'm the bad guy. Thanks for making my job harder.

What just happened here?

As it turns out, the dad was raised by a very strict disciplinarian who ran the house like a military academy. Punishment was swift and serious. He was never allowed to cry without being shamed or humiliated. He doesn't want his son to have the experience he had growing up.

The mom, raised by parents who lacked consistent rules, never knew what to expect. Sometimes doing something was fine, sometimes it drew outbursts of shouting and blame or rage. She created a set of fixed rules to help her—and her children—feel stable and predictable.

Of course, people don't always raise their kids in the exact opposite way they were raised.

Sometimes, the laid-back parent was raised by laid-back parents and the strict disciplinarian was raised that way too. One way or another, childhood experiences shape the way we parent our children. You may think one parent was right and one was wrong in the cookie story (based on your own Core Values) but the important lesson here is to recognize that this couple hadn't shared their Personal Core Values with each other. If they had, they would've known what each other valued. That conversation would have been much different!

Knowing your Personal Core Values will benefit your parenting decisions right away, so let's dive in. I recommend setting aside at least 30 minutes for this exercise, but many people take longer. Follow your heart and honor your process, however it feels best for you.

Exercise: Identifying Your Personal Core Values

Think about each of these questions and write down the words that come to mind:

1. What's important to me? What matters deeply to me?
2. What character traits are the most important to me?
3. What words describe my deepest beliefs?
4. What are the principles I fight for in an argument?
5. What organizations do I support or what causes do I champion?

______________________	______________________
______________________	______________________
______________________	______________________
______________________	______________________
______________________	______________________

How does your list look?

Does it accurately reflect you?

It's okay if you have five words or fifteen words at this stage. We may be adding a few more and whittling the list down. Some people feel pressure to come up with suitable words unprompted. Below is a list of top Core Values to get you started.

When you see a word that triggers anger or frustration, think about its opposite as a potential Core Value. (Also make a note so you can dig deeper into why it holds so much power over you.)

Don't select a word because you think it's better than another word—there are no points given out for a list that looks amazing.

Many women admit in their first attempt at selecting words, they picked traits they knew their partners would like, not words that were truly self-reflective. Be mindful that 'who you are' and 'who you want to be' are at the heart of this exercise, not 'who you have been' or 'who you think you should be.'

Both men and women report that this exercise was the first time they thought about themselves in this way and though it may feel awkward to put yourself in the center for the exercise, it's critical to quiet your mind and dig deep into your heart and soul. Select what is most important in your life for your fulfillment, joy, bliss, meaning, and purpose. If there are some words that pop into mind that are not here, please add them because this is your list!

Also, words have dictionary meanings, but they also have cultural and geographical significances so feel free to select words that mean what you believe them to mean.

Without overthinking, select 5-10 words that resonate deeper than others.

Personal Core Value List

Ability	Daring	Humor	Persistent
Acceptance	Decisive	Impact	Philanthropy
Accessibility	Dependable	Impartial	Play
Accomplished	Determined	Independent	Positive
Accurate	Diligent	Innovative	Practical
Achievement	Dutiful	Inquisitive	Prepared
Adventure	Education	Inspiring	Private
Ambition	Efficient	Integrity	Productive
Appreciation	Empathetic	Intelligent	Realistic
Assertive	Encouraging	Intuitive	Reliable
Authentic	Energetic	Joy	Resilient
Authority	Entrepreneur	Justice	Resourceful
Balance	Environmental	Kindness	Results-focus
Beauty	Ethical	Knowledge	Religion
Bold	Excellence	Lawful	Reputation
Brave	Fair	Leadership	Respect
Calm	Faith	Learning	Responsible
Capable	Family	Listening	Self-Respect
Careful	Fearless	Logical	Service
Challenger	Flexible	Love	Spirituality
Charitable	Freedom	Loyalty	Simplicity
Cleanliness	Friendships	Meticulous	Stability
Collaborative	Fun	Mindful	Status
Community	Generosity	Nature	Success
Compassion	Grace	Openness	Thoughtful
Competent	Gratitude	Optimism	Traditional
Competitive	Happiness	Order	Trustworthy
Contribution	Hard working	Organized	Truth
Cooperation	Health	Patient	Understanding
Courageous	Helpful	Patriotic	Unique
Creative	Honesty	Peace	Wealth
Curious	Hopeful	Pleasure	Wisdom

After you have selected your words, write them below, including the words you may have come up with on your own from the **Identifying Your Personal Core Values Exercise**.

______________________________	______________________________
______________________________	______________________________
______________________________	______________________________
______________________________	______________________________
______________________________	______________________________

Look at your list for a few moments, one word at a time.

For each one, think about how it makes you feel. What images or thoughts come to your mind when you see that word? Are there themes? Maybe you selected a few words that mean the same thing? Make a note of that here.

When you've reflected on each word, go back through the list and circle your top ten. Select words that really resonate with you, made you smile, or gave a sense of comfort or joy.

______________________________	______________________________
______________________________	______________________________
______________________________	______________________________
______________________________	______________________________
______________________________	______________________________

Reread your list and make sure they feel good.

Now, pick the top 5-7 that absolutely define you. Words that if someone heard the list, they would know it described you. I know it's hard to pick your top favorites from a *list* of favorites, but you can do it!

To help you select your true Personal Core Values, reflect on these questions:

How deeply does this define me or choices I've made?

How hard would I fight for this value?

Do I consider this essential to my life?

Does this represent my main way of being in the world?

Chances are, after pondering each of these questions, you can remove another word or two from this list. If you're feeling hesitant or resistant, go back to the initial super list. See if you'd like to swap out any of your top ten choices for one that might have slipped through the cracks the first time. Oftentimes, this can help you return to your list of ten with a fresh perspective. You may have an easier time removing 2-3 that are amazing, but not *core* values.

When you're happy with your top words, write them down.

____________________ ____________________

____________________ ____________________

____________________ ____________________

Congratulations on undertaking this critical exercise!

When we have a clearly defined set of Personal Core Values, we avoid making decisions that go against who we want to be. It gives us the courage to say yes when we mean yes, and no when we mean no.

As the first step in laying the foundation for the Five Elements of Awareness, knowing your Core Values will guide your rules, routines, structures, and systems as you travel along your parenting journey.

If you skipped the exercise above, don't worry. Your kids will still inherit your value system. They will integrate it into their lives without even knowing it—that's legacy learning in action! Just be aware that if you haven't completed the Personal Core Value exercise, you might give your child values that are part of your history, but not ones you'd like to carry into the future. Knowing who you are and what you stand for means you'll prioritize the things that matter the most.

Sharing Your List

Once you and your partner have created your own Personal Core Values lists, it's time to share them with each other. Keep this a relaxed and unhurried conversation.

Simply talking about your Core Values in one conversation isn't enough. In the heat of the moment when your deepest beliefs are challenged, you may forget your partner's values are different from your own.

Let's see this in action.

In the Spencer family, every two hours that fifteen-year old Kayla is out with friends, she must text her parents a picture showing where she is and who she is with. One night, she sent a dark, blurry picture. She was dancing on her friend's back porch. Her parents each receive the text while at home. Kayla's dad, Steve, yelled at his wife.

Steve: Jeni, look at your phone! Is this a joke? What's going on with Kayla?

Jeni: Oh, cute.

Steve: Cute? She chopped off her hair and dyed it purple. Did you know?

Jeni: No.

Steve: Did she tell you she was planning to do this?

Jeni: No, but girls often experiment with their looks.

Steve: How can you say that? Call her and get her home right now. She's grounded. She's lost her freedom, phone, that party she wants to go to, everything!

Jeni: Honey, what's going on? It's just hair. Why are you so fired up?

Steve: Why am I fired up? The question is why aren't *you* fired up? Our fifteen-year old does whatever she likes without checking with me first. You act like it's no big deal! Who does she think she is?

She's obviously not old enough to use good judgment. I'll have to make all her decisions for her!

Jeni: *Deep breath. Thinking quickly*. Sweetie, remember we took that parenting course last month and learned about Core Values? One of your strongest words was authority. What if you aren't really upset about her hair? What if you're upset that she didn't ask first? Could that be it?

Steve: What? That course doesn't matter. I'm focused on how ridiculous she looks.

Jeni: What if it washes out in a week? We don't know. Let's tell her we need to know before she makes these decisions next time because this feels disrespectful.

Steve: It's totally disrespectful! I would never have done this to my parents- they would've taken out the belt! What's next with her experimenting? Nose piercings and tattoos? Or are you fine with those too since you don't care she's out of control?

PING.

A new text. They both look at their phones to see Kayla with her long, blond hair flowing around her shoulders. Her friend is now wearing the short, purple wig.

Steve: What the ... it's not even real.

Jeni: It's okay, honey. Look, it's ok.

Steve: What just happened? I can't believe it.

> We sat in that workshop listening to parents who exploded at their kids and I dismissed them as raging lunatics. Kayla just hit my hot button and *I* was that raging lunatic! I'm so glad she wasn't here. I could've really destroyed our relationship. It just hit me so fast.
>
> Jeni: Yes, it did.
>
> Steve: Wait, I yelled at you too! I insinuated there was something wrong with you because you weren't as furious as I was, but you saw her experimenting, you didn't see her disrespecting us like I did. Wow, I've got some pretty deep authority issues to face. I'm so sorry.

In this story, Kayla inadvertently challenged her father's top Core Value. Had she been home, their relationship would have gone from Summer to Winter in the blink of an eye. As a bystander, you can see that just because Steve was triggered doesn't mean the mom was equally enraged—or even that the child was wrong.

Kayla's unexpected challenge to her dad's core belief generated a tsunami of emotion for him. It would have taken a lot of work to repair the damage to their bond. When Jeni mentioned the workshop, she remembered that authority and respect were his highest values. In the moment, her husband dismissed it. One of the main reasons he brushed it aside was because they didn't use their lists as the starting point to blend both parent's Core Value lists together to create a Family Value List.

It's not hard to make decisions when you know what your values are.

~ Roy E. Disney,
nephew of Walt Disney

CHAPTER 9

Element Two: Family Values

....

What are Family Values?

Family Values are a collection of agreed-upon words or phrases that guide the priorities, rules, and decisions of your whole family.

They're created by the parents with potential input from the children.[vii]

Although it's similar to a mission statement, Family Values can capture many different ideas that are important to your family. It doesn't need to have one main focus. As we learned from Jeni, Steve, and Kayla's purple wig, identifying your Core Values isn't enough, we need to use our Core Values to create a parenting plan for our family highlighting what matters most to us as a group and we need to be on the same page for times of struggle or conflict. It's

vii Please note that involving children work best when there is openness and equality between the parents. If there is an imbalance, any control issues, codependency, or unresolved trauma, collaboration isn't going to happen the same for you. I strongly encourage you to seek professional help first to establish more of a partnership between the adults before a family value system be formed, especially before getting input from the kids. My heart is with you on your journey.

critical to use the Personal Core Value lists to build a unified and blended collection of values that highlight and celebrate items from both parent's lists.

Let's jump right in.

Creating Your Family Values

Take two sheets of paper, and on the first write Family Values.

Take the second sheet and fold it in half. List your Core Values on one half of the sheet and your partner's Core Values on the other half.[viii]

Are there overlapping beliefs or duplications?

Let's say, for example, you both value philanthropy. Cross that word out on each of your lists and write it on the first sheet you titled Family Values.

Now we can explore what's left.

I recommend both partners share their list in a relaxed manner on a relaxed day because listening and holding space is critical. For each word, take time to explain the history, the meaning, and why it is so profound. When the first person is done with their whole list, invite the listening partner to co-select a few words to add to the Family Value List on the other sheet.

Now, change roles.

The speaker is now the listener, and the second parent will share their personal core value list, explaining the history, meaning,

---

viii If you are a single parent, please still complete this exercise because the Family Values List contains phrases that expand on the single-word entries of your Personal Core Value list, and this list is family-focused.

and why it is so profound. The speaker can then invite the listening parent to co-select some words to add to the Family Values on the other sheet.

This exercise accomplishes a few things.

First, it gives both parents the time and space to share experiences that both shaped them from a young age and continue to guide their decisions, understanding, preferences, and actions. Being open, honest, and vulnerable allows the bond between you to deepen significantly.

Second, it allows you to see where there is alignment, or shared values, as well as where there is misalignment, or potential for hurt, disappointment, anger, or frustration. Couples often report that completing this exercise improved their relationship as well as their relationships with their kids.

Third, it blends values that you both hold dear to create a family legacy, or a way of life, that will weave through the choices your children make.

Once you've agreed on common values from your personal lists, decide if you'd like to include your children in the next step: brainstorming.

Invite Your Children

Sitting down with your children and opening this conversation up may seem daunting, but taken in age-appropriate chunks, it's an empowering exercise.

It could take a few meetings to finalize your list, so enjoy the process however it unfolds. Feel free to share the master Core

Values List from earlier in this chapter and your Personal Core Values lists so your children can see what traits you and your partner value the most.

With kids of any age, questions help stimulate their thoughts. I recommend you write everything down to capture it in the moment. You can edit later.

Some questions for kids may include:

- What are the most important things in our family?
- What are our strengths?
- What words describe us best?
- What can you count on with our family?
- What do you love most about us?
- What do we do *really* well?
- How does our family handle conflict or challenges?

Your family list should reflect your family.

If you're an adventurous family, your list should reflect adventure or an openness and willingness for new experiences. If you're a spiritual family, your list should reflect spiritual practices, traditions, and rituals. If you are a playful family, your list should reflect spontaneity, spirited activities, movement, and enthusiastic living.

Since you have completed your Personal Core Value List, you can guide your children on selecting words that feel right. I wanted to share some phrases other families have embraced for their Family Values to get you started:

- Prioritize play.
- Create freely.
- Do something you love every day.
- Treat everybody else with compassion.
- Always do your personal best.
- Be open to new experiences as long as they are safe.
- Be a lifelong learner and make education a priority.
- Celebrate everyone's big and small successes.
- Use money to do things, rather than to buy things.
- Take care of Mother Earth, plants and animals.

Once your list of 5-10 Family Values are identified (you can keep them as words or phrases), display them so your family can see and think about them throughout the day.

After a week or so, hold another family meeting to review. Do they really describe your family? Is there some tweaking to do? Is there another idea that should be considered?

Once you have finalized your Family Values, prominently display it somewhere central so it can become a powerful tool. It can guide discussions, arguments, struggle points, and negotiations on your path to Summer.

Troubleshooting the List

Tameka realized that creating the list is only one part of the list's power.

Her family of six worked diligently over a period of two months to craft a beautiful, unique list. They even had a celebration at the end with cake and candles. Tameka wanted to frame and hang it, but life got busy. Their unframed list ended up under some mail and sat for a few weeks.

In the meantime, her kids bickered and barked. She was losing patience.

She called me, frustrated and worried that they had spent so much time crafting this list and it wasn't working. I asked her where it was being displayed. She went silent.

In a pile.

At the bottom.

Hidden from sight and out of mind.

I instructed her to find it and hang it up right away in their kitchen, frame or no frame. I asked if she would be open to start her weekly family meeting by reading their Family Values to keep it fresh in everyone's minds before schedules, conflicts, or discussions took precedence.

She called me a week later totally elated—it had worked!

> You won't believe what I heard in the kitchen when I was making dinner the other night. I heard four kids out-yelling each other, louder and louder to get their voices heard. My youngest daughter Lacey clapped her hands a few times. When they stopped screaming at each other, that little girl reminded her older brothers that one of our Family Values is *Honor Each Other When Speaking.* They needed to respect each other better when

> one person was talking. Two of my boys started to tease her. She walked right over to the chart on the wall and pointed it out, with all our signatures on it. She said, "You signed this! Was making our family better a joke to you?" Those boys were silent and I was so proud! I hoped it would help me as a mom but I didn't realize how powerful it would be for them to build confidence and respect with each other. Thank you!
>
> ***~ Tameka, mother of five***

Tameka thought their work was done when they created the list, but that was just part of it. The real influence happens when your Family Value List becomes part of your vocabulary, daily routine, integrated into conversations and discussions, and used when your family is headed into Fall or Winter.

When we proclaim our Core Values and Family Values out loud and hang them for all to see, your kids will use them to find their voice, power, or confidence, just like Tameka's daughter Lacey. As they age, these values will become a part of the fabric of who they are and how they live their life, which is an amazing and powerful gift.

It would be great if investing in your Family Values List is a one-and-done deal, but it isn't set in stone like your Personal Core Values. Your Family Values List is there to guide your choices, commitments, decisions, and actions. Your list may eventually feel like an old pair of pants that tugs in new places. As your family evolves, your Family Values List can change to keep serving everyone.

Your Family Values List sets the tone for your family. It can be used as the foundation for setting goals and daily priorities. For example, let's say you have *Move our bodies in fun ways to stay healthy and strong* on your Family Values List. You'll create goals and set priorities to support that value. Creating goals and priorities are critical life skills that are part of the Five Elements of Awareness, and we'll dive into them next.

> *Things which matter most must never be at the mercy of things which matter least.*
> ***~ Johann Wolfgang von Goethe, Author***

CHAPTER 10

Element Three: Goals and Priorities

. . . .

Family Goals

Once upon a long-time ago, after our three kids finally fell asleep, my husband and I collapsed on the sofa to binge watch a few episodes of our recent obsession. We zoned out, exhausted. Without using complete sentences, we gathered enough strength to blurt out things like:

> "National Park free day next month. We going?"
> "Campsites opening up for July. Yeah?"
> "Kid's birthday parties, anywhere specific?"

We floated from topic to topic, finding bits and pieces to fill our summer calendar. But like the previous year—and the year before that—we didn't commit to anything. We got a bit snippy in our chat, then put on the show and left our plans unresolved.

In all honesty, I wanted to do great things with the kids and more than anything I wanted to introduce them to Europe—but I hesitated because all of the *planning and doing* would fall on me. Europe is a big place filled with endless options for adventure and memory-making but I just didn't have the time or the energy to research dozens of destinations to pick the best one, and then do the actual planning for where to stay, what to see, and what to do.

Then, something awesome happened.

A few nights later, I casually mentioned that I wasn't sure if we would have our dream European vacation because it was a lot of work to even figure out where to go. Our youngest went to his room and returned with his globe. He spun it slowly, studying it, and then his face lit up when his little finger found the city.

Paris.

All of a sudden, we had Paris.

Excitement about this trip grew immediately, partly because it was *Paris*, yes, but partly because a dream was going to come true. Over the years, we had read books set in Paris, seen the Eiffel Tower in movies, and after a small roundabout was installed in our city, I showed the kids an online video of the most intense roundabout I had ever seen located around the Arc de Triomphe.

Once we had our destination, we all invested in researching the coolest parks, the nicest views, and the best pastry shops in the city and our dream came true because we had something specific to focus on and work towards.

That is the power of setting a goal.

'Would you tell me, please,
which way I ought to go from here?'
'That depends a good deal on where you want to get
to,' said the Cat.
'I don't much care where--' said Alice.
'Then it doesn't matter which way you go,' said the Cat.

~ from "Alice in Wonderland"
by Lewis Carroll

Why Set Goals?

Family Goals are a way to breathe life into our Family Values through our choices and how we spend our resources, like time, money, and energy.

Creating Family Goals gives your family the opportunity to dream together. Setting goals, whether big or small, shifts everyone into a proactive mindset. It takes you off autopilot and allows you to live your Family Values. Moving towards your family goal gives everyone the opportunity to practice decision-making, cooperation, and compromise. And, reaching your goal lets you all celebrate this great accomplishment together.

Research shows that the act of planning is the single best technique to reduce stress.[20]

If the idea of setting goals sounds overwhelming, don't worry—you probably already do it without knowing.

For example, say your child wants to try out for the school play but you know *dreaming isn't doing* so you help him. You help him fill out his application, give him pointers as he selects a monologue, and encourage him to practice every night. His goal was to be cast in the play and all of his actions helped him reach his goal. Family Goals are the same way but they include and benefit the family.

Creating and committing to a goal means you're deciding it will be done.

Dr. Gail Matthews, a psychology professor at the Dominican University in California, recently studied the art and science of goal setting. She surveyed 267 people and split them into two groups: those who wrote down their goals and dreams, and those who didn't. She found that we are 42% more likely to achieve our goals by writing them down on a regular basis. That number goes up if you have a goal, write it down, and share with someone who believes in you. [21]

There are regular goals—which are simple and open-to-interpretation—and then there are S.M.A.R.T. goals.

The S.M.A.R.T. Goal Setting System[ix]

The S.M.A.R.T. technique was initially created for corporations, but this system easily supports personal goals. The structure is easy and clear and designed to move from goal-set to goal-success. The basic premise is to have clearly defined parameters to attain success, so every goal must be:

ix There are many established Goal Setting Strategies, but in my experience working with families and children, this system is the clearest and easiest to create, track and follow. Feel free to use whatever goal-setting system that helps you reach your dream outcome.

S – Specific (Who, what, where, when, why?)
M – Measurable (How to know it's reached?)
A – Achievable (Can we accomplish this goal?)
R – Relevant (Is it aligned with all our goals?)
T – Timely (When will this goal be completed?)

Here's an example of a regular goal:

Our family will do some community service together.

Now let's put that through the S.M.A.R.T. system:

Our family will volunteer at the food bank for two hours on the first Tuesday of the month during June, July, and August.

Specific: who (we), what (volunteer), when (Tues/Jun-Aug)
Measurable: signing up to volunteer 3X, pledge is logged
Achievable: by volunteering 6 hours, goal is achieved
Relevant: Family Values include doing community service
Timely: it will be completed the first Tuesday in Aug

When we set a goal in our family, it can be hit or miss if it happens. But when we work together to set a S.M.A.R.T. goal, very little can stand in our way. Having a clearly defined, specific outcome is key here. When you have enough details, the process and outcome is crystal clear.

If your daughter says, "Let's go camping!" you can ask:

Mountains? Riverside? Lakeside? Meadow? Beach? Tent camping? Cabins? Bonfires? Boating? Hiking?

The more she can paint the picture in her mind, the closer you are to having all you need to set a S.M.A.R.T. goal.

How to Create a Family Goal:

Brainstorm All Ideas

Set out some large paper or sticky notes and invite everyone to a brainstorming session.

Together, create a list of cool ideas that your family could work toward and encourage your kids to dream as big as their imagination can go. Record all the ideas without filtering. (If *Going into Space* is suggested, add that too! You can visit the space museum or go star-gazing! #makeitwork)

You and your partner should be the last to add your ideas. Your kids may not offer their suggestions if they feel that you'll pick your own ideas anyway.

Select One Goal

It might feel a bit intoxicating to jump on all your brainstormed ideas with zest and zeal, but in the beginning, dear friend, let's go slow.

Don't overwhelm or burn anyone out! When everyone has contributed, you and your partner can review the ideas. Refer to your Core Values and your Family Value List and select one that aligns best. There may be other awesome goals on the list, but the timing might not be right. That's ok! You can keep this list forever.

Some examples could include:

- Vacation in a specific place.
- Plant a backyard garden.
- Conquer a challenging hike.
- Learn a new sport or activity.
- Build a tree house.

Identify Obstacles

This step may be done with or without the children, but the idea is to identify things that may block your success. Constraints on time, money, or access (space travel, anyone?) are common blocks.

If possible, come up with solutions to each obstacle so that you increase your chances of making it happen.

Say for example your family goal is to go to Disney World. You might identify one obstacle as a lack of money. This was our situation when our kids were much younger, but we didn't want to give up our goal. We came up with cost-saving measures like:

- Buying inexpensive Disney souvenirs throughout the year that we brought with us on our trip to give to our kids instead of spending a fortune in the Disney stores there.
- Staying in a hotel off the main property that had a kitchen so we could fuel up on a big breakfast and evening snacks.
- Buying our tickets during a holiday sale, even though we weren't traveling for months.

List Your Resources

Even if you feel stuck without many options, you are more resource-rich than you think!

Start making a list of the things you could use to help reach your goal. This list could include people you know casually, friends, friends of friends, online resources, search engines, websites, products, workshops, specialists, and online groups where you can find the tools, guidance and/or skills you need.

Set a Timeline

There are many kinds of goals. Some can be met in the short-term (set up a movie marathon in two weeks), and some of them take longer (buy a camper van next year).

Many families pick a short-term goal first so they can go through the process quickly, testing it out in the real-world of their family. Whatever you choose, select a goal you can all rally behind, work towards, and accomplish together.

Make a Step-by-step Plan

With your goal in mind, list out every single step, big or small, from the very first step until you arrive at the last step, which can be *Celebrate Reaching Our Goal!*

On your list, be mindful to write each one in its smallest action item possible, like *print a tourist map for Central Park with points of interest* instead of *get map*.

Beside each step, identify possible obstacles and list known resources so you can see where you may need to problem-solve to keep moving forward.

Share It with Everyone

Now comes the fun part!

Your family has come up with a wonderful goal to work towards, you've itemized the steps, identified and problem-solved possible challenges, and now you get to work towards your goal!

Share it, talk about it, dream about it, and encourage your kids to share their vision of how it will feel when they reach it. Their enthusiasm can blow you away! If they're younger, or your goal is longer term, review the steps with your children, and then return to it regularly. Check where you are and how you're doing to meet your commitments.

If you find something isn't working or moving your family forward, adjust the steps to keep you on track.

Some families make a visual timeline or a checklist to keep the momentum strong. This is also the perfect time to delegate small tasks to your kids to keep them connected to the outcome.

Once your family successfully reaches its goal, you might feel inspired to set a few goals simultaneously—that's awesome! Some families select a short-term and a long-term goal, and others set monthly goals and an annual goal. As soon as you have a few goals on the go, it's time to prioritize.

Priorities

We have to get real here.

There will never be enough of you to go around. As busy parents, you'll make choices over and over as to what gets your attention and energy. It's normal in the stress of a moment to pick the low hanging fruit or grease the squeaky wheel, but we need to set our priorities based on our Core Values, Family Values, and our Family Goals to really connect with our kids and build the life of our dreams.

Although goals and priorities are sometimes interchanged, they are not the same thing. A goal is something you set for your future. A priority is what you do daily or weekly to keep you on the right path toward your goal.

If you have a Family Value of *Exercise in Fun Ways*, your family might set a goal to run a family-friendly 5K fundraiser with a cause near and dear to your hearts. To reach your goal, you would prioritize buying new running shoes and jogging with your children three times a week in preparation.

Setting priorities is a life skill and an important one. When we know what we want to focus on, we make sure we have time for it. Hopefully it's something that can positively impact our lives!

Now seems like a good time to look at your to-do list. Prioritize your most important items, delete all non-essentials, and make room for new priorities that will arise after goal setting with your children.

You'll definitely have priorities in your life that aren't attached to a Family Goal, that's to be expected. We juggle hundreds of things each week, so in order to have time and energy to pursue a fun Family Goal, we need to make sure we're only doing important, necessary things.

Let's write down the top ten burning, critical things on your to-do list right now. (I know you can think of 75 things, but we'll start small!)

______________________	______________________
______________________	______________________
______________________	______________________
______________________	______________________
______________________	______________________

Now ask yourself the following questions:

- What has low value/low importance?
- What can you eliminate right now?
- What can you finish in under ten minutes?
- What is blocking you from getting other items done? (Money? Procrastinating? Waiting for more information?)

Looking at what is left on your list, circle the top three things most impactful for you, your partner, or your children. Commit to working on those in the next week. Allow the other items to sit happily at the bottom of the list for another time.

Now you have some openings in your calendar for priorities toward supporting your family goal.

Your priorities are a roadmap for your life. They illuminate the path to your goal at the end of the road. When you have your priorities ranked from most important to least important, it's easy to make decisions or say yes or no to new ideas or commitments. Your map will tell you if your decision will keep you moving toward your goal, or off into the weeds.

The Family Values List and your Family Goals focus on the whole picture, but it's time we come down to eye level of the most important people in our lives—our children.

They come with their own unique personality, which plays a big role in the decisions we make, the projects we commit to, and the overall happiness in our lives.

The time has come to talk about temperament.

CHAPTER 11

Element Four: Temperament

• • • • • • •

Temperament is a set of traits your child was born with that helps him organize the world around him.

In Chapter 4, we learned that happiness expert Dr. Lyubomirsky believes 50% of our happiness comes from our genetically predetermined natural temperament, or the way we're wired to understand the world around us.

Why is this important?

It's critical to understand your child's unique traits so you can nurture and support their innate needs, or go with their natural and predetermined flow, to stay in a Summer relationship.

Knowing your child's temperament can help you understand how your child will react in different situations. You can use this to help him find success and strengthen skills that might not be fully developed. The more you know about your child, the stronger the chances are that you can guide your family to be in a state of Summer and stay there.

The Nine Temperamental Traits

American child psychologist Dr. Stella Chess and her husband Dr. Alexander Thomas spearheaded a classic New York Longitudinal study in the early 1950s. They tracked hundreds of children over a thirty-year period to understand the tendencies babies are born with and how these tendencies influence their lives. From that research they developed the 9 Temperamental Traits.[22]

The traits for your child are:

Activity Level: how active is he most of the time?
Distractibility: how easily is she distracted?
Intensity: how intense is his responses?
Regularity: does she vary in her eating/sleeping habits?
Sensory Threshold: how sensitive is he to physical touch?
Approach/Withdrawal: response to strangers?
Adaptability: how easily does she adapt to changes?
Persistence: how long will he try to solve something hard?
Mood: is he a glass half empty or half full kind of person?

As I read through this list, I think about conversations I have with moms of newborns. Some of the first things they say point to their baby's temperaments—even though they might not be aware of them.

> "She's such an easy baby. She will go to anyone, unlike my son who only wanted me and would scream bloody murder if someone else picked

> him up."

> "He's a mess if he isn't in bed at 11 for his nap. Seriously, the entire day is ruined if his schedule shifts even a bit."

> "You know that toy that has different shaped holes and you can only put the star shape in the star hole and the circle shape in the circle hole? As a toddler, my oldest daughter would sit for at least an hour every day pushing colored shape blocks through their corresponding holes. She would grunt when they didn't fit and laugh hysterically when they went through. My youngest might sit for ten seconds, get frustrated, and throw the shapes at the cat."

This study was designed to monitor what temperamental traits babies exhibited and how those traits evolved (or didn't evolve) as the child grew. Think back to your own children's newborn period. Within the first few months, you can see that your child was probably showing you who he was in his response to things around him. As your child aged, you may not have stopped to think about how he adapted to changes in his day, or how long he worked at something difficult unless it was pointed out by a coach or a teacher.

So why is knowing your child's temperament important?

Let's say your mornings are the worst.

You wake up every work day with a sense of dread. Getting your child ready for school is the hardest part of the day. You come to her room, flip on her light, and tell her it's time to get ready. You leave, shower, dress, and you pop back in. She may still be in bed or maybe she's sitting on the floor, rearranging her stuffed bears. You firmly instruct her to get ready.

You make lunches, start breakfast, brew coffee, wipe the counter, notice the time is already getting late, and you go back to her room. She is back in bed, reading an old comic you bought her months ago. You lose it with her and tell her she's sabotaging your mornings again—you just want it to be easy! She starts to cry, you feel horrible, and the saddest thing is knowing this will happen a few more times this week.

What if you knew your child was hardwired to be highly distractible? Could that be a game changer?

Of course!

You could start with one change that would end your dread: a morning routine.

Imagine this in a new way.

Before she goes to bed, help her look at her schedule for the next day. You both pick out an outfit and gather everything she'll need on her floor near her bag. You wake up thirty minutes earlier than your usual time in the morning, set some intentions for a wonderful day, stretch, shower, dress, and then you wake her up gently and slowly.

You leave for a few minutes to start breakfast. When you come back, you remove a clipboard from its hook on her wall and sit beside her to review it together.

> Stand up, stretch. Wake up your body.
>
> Use the restroom.
>
> Take off pajamas, put them under pillow.
>
> Put on the outfit we selected yesterday.
>
> Pull up your blanket to make your bed.
>
> Brush your hair.
>
> Come to the kitchen to eat breakfast.
>
> Pack your lunch in your bag.
>
> Brush your teeth.
>
> Hugs! Kisses! Have a great day!

By giving her a tool to stay focused on morning tasks, you've transformed your day and your morning to be a pleasant and positive experience.

If you know your child is curious and determined, you won't tell her not to stick her toys in the electrical outlets. You'll install safety covers and use furniture to cut off her access.

If you know your child has a low sensory threshold, you can be aware of the fabrics you buy for his bedding and clothes.

Knowing their temperament is vital to having an environment that supports them, instead of one that sabotages them.

At this point, you're probably going back in your mind to think about your child's behaviors to figure out her temperament.

We can do it together.

Exercise: Discovering Temperament

Below, I have created a chart to help you evaluate your children and their unique characteristics. Remember, there is no right or wrong, good or bad. Each child brings many different talents and gifts to the world—that's ok!

As an example, here's a chart from Michelle and Nick, parents of three boys:

	child 1	**child 2**	**child 3**
activity	very	a bit	a bit
distractibility	very	a bit	not really
intensity	very	very	not really
regularity	not really	very	not really
sensory	not really	not really	very
approach	open	closed	closed
adaptability	very	a bit	very
persistence	very	a bit	very
mood	optimistic	pessimistic	optimistic

Now it's your turn!

	Child 1	Child 2	Child 3
Activity			
Distractibility			
Intensity			
Regularity			
Sensory			
Approach			
Adaptability			
Persistence			
Mood			
	Child 4	**Child 5**	**Child 6**
Activity			
Distractibility			
Intensity			
Regularity			
Sensory			
Approach			
Adaptability			
Persistence			
Mood			

How Temperament Impacts Parenting

Let's look at Michelle and Nick's chart again.

Their first and third kids are more *glass half full* and *adaptable* kind of people, while their middle child is cautious, resistant to change, and more worried that things might go wrong.

That's completely okay *and* this helps them know that when split-second decisions are being made, they will need to pay greater attention to their middle child.

When they were in Whistler last summer (a Canadian mountain resort north of Vancouver), they decided to surprise the kids with a day trip to a nearby high-ropes course where they could pretend to be Tarzan, walking on ropes and swinging into nets high in the treetops while harnessed to a safety wire.

Their oldest and youngest were over-the-moon excited, but their middle son didn't want to go. He refused to eat breakfast, wouldn't get dressed, and was worried he would fall or get hurt.

As a former teacher, I have seen this before. Over the years, I've heard parents say these kinds of statements when their child doesn't jump on board right away:

- "Don't you make me come and make you get ready."
- "You better not make us late."
- "You should be grateful we got you one at all."
- "For once can just do it without causing problems?"
- "Why do we even bother doing nice things for you?"
- "Stop being so difficult."

These parents are often frustrated because they think their child is resisting on purpose. Actually, resistance is often a sign that the child needs more information, support, or control.

When you learn about your child's temperament, resistance and other outwardly behaviors will not be simply what they seem. They will be a gateway to understanding something deeper within your child. One question you can ask yourself is this: what purpose does this behavior serve?

In Nick and Michelle's situation, their son saying *no* was an invitation for more information, an indicator he was afraid.

In our conversation, Nick made the connection that in many of their family activities, their middle child needed to know more than his brothers about the scope of the activity, the ins and outs, the start time, the end time, and everything in between. Sometimes they gave him more and sometimes they dismissed his questions. Those were the times that their son resisted or withdrew. By the end of our conversation, Nick realized he needed to parent them differently based on their temperament.

Here is another example of how temperament can impact our parenting. My first and second child are intense and passionate (hmmm... they are both Leo's!) while my third is more reserved and internal.

When my older two start ramping up or become hyper-excited, the volume shoots up. The energy around them becomes electric. In these instances, I purposefully check on my youngest because I know it's overwhelming for him. As a toddler, when he heard them getting louder, he would hide. Everyone would stop and wonder what happened to him. Then we figured it out.

He felt anxious when the environment became intense.

He's now older and knows to tell them that he's going to walk away because they're becoming too much. Sometimes they ignore him and dig in deeper, or sometimes they see it from his perspective and go to their rooms to cool off.

Knowing your child's temperament is a critical piece of the parenting puzzle. When you know how your child naturally experiences the world, you can meet their needs and maintain a connected, warm Summer relationship. Now that we know all about our children's temperaments, it's time to understand what the best method is to connect with your unique child.

CHAPTER 12

Element Five: Communication Style

•••••••

F*ortunately, best-selling authors Dr.* Gary Chapman and Dr. Ross Campbell wrote The 5 Love Languages for Children. In this book, they outline the five main ways that we give or receive love. According to Dr. Chapman, everyone has one main love language and one secondary love language that describes how we best feel love, even though we may give or receive love in all five ways. The five love languages that help us deeply connect to our children are:

Gifts: Small, meaningful gifts show your care and appreciation, like a heart-shaped rock, a fun pair of socks, gum in a new flavor, or a handmade photo frame.

Quality Time: Dedicated, uninterrupted time with your child playing a game, exploring, taking a class together, or eating out.

Words of Affirmation: Kind and thoughtful words of encouragement and support written on little notecards, hidden in their lunch, texted, or old-fashioned speaking.

Acts of Service: Doing something for them to help them when they need TLC—like breakfast in bed, fixing a broken toy, or helping with chores.

Physical Touch: Active play can be wrestling, physical games, or tickling. Gentle play can be a massage, cuddling during a movie, reading, or thumb wars.

Speaking your child's love language is the key to reaching their heart and keeping your relationship in Summer. The kind, loving things you do will be recognized as expressions of love and appreciated the most. The lines of communication and the threads of connection will strengthen.

Discovering Your Child's Preferred Communication Style

When thinking about my kids, I thought to myself, "Yes, they love gifts. They always want to be with me. They love to hear ways I love them. I'm often serving their needs. And yes, they like to cuddle. They want them all!"

One way to find the more dominant communication style for our children is to observe them with these questions in mind:

1. How does my child express love to me?
2. How does my child express love to others?
3. What does my child ask for the most?
4. What does my child complain about the most?

When I went through this exercise a few years back, it wasn't easy to determine their top two love languages. Now that my kids are older, it has become clearer.

As with every exercise in this book, looking at each child separately creates the opportunity for the greatest success.

My oldest wants to talk to me, day and night. He finds me when I'm working, cooking, or exercising, and tells me about his day, his thoughts, his struggles, and his ideas. His top love language? Words of Affirmation.

My middle child spent most of her young life crafting with me and she still often surprises me with pretty cards she covered in calligraphy and glitter so I thought it might be gifts but she loves to scrapbook with me, she joins me when I run errands, and she finds me to show me funny videos. Her top love language? Quality time.

My youngest needs to be close. If he's reading, he will sit rightbesideme with no room to wiggle. At dinner, if the other two kids take the seats near me, he will sit right across from me and touch my foot with his foot, often without really being conscious of it. His top preference is Physical Touch.

There isn't a set age when your children might show you their preferences. Some kids show you at a younger age and some kids show you at a later age. Either way is totally normal!

You can find your child's love language by taking Dr. Chapman's quiz at www.5lovelanguages.com.

You can also play with me here. I created an unscientific and experimental exercise you can do in the comfort of your life to help identify which rise to the top, and which fall to the bottom.

Quick Reference Guide for Summer & Winter

	The path to Summer	The path to Winter
Gifts	Thoughtfulness expressed with meaningful gifts to show them that you care.	Forgetting special events. Buying something without meaning or thoughtfulness.
Quality Time	Scheduling time together without distractions or interruptions, a full 100% of your attention.	Not being present when together, or not showing up at all. Staying in big groups so there is no special time for you two.
Words of Affirmation	Sharing words of encouragement, support, and appreciation through speaking or sending a note, text, or card.	Non-constructive criticism, using harsh words, sarcasm or snarkiness to make your point. Using words as weapons.
Acts of Service	Offering to help with chores or homework, or things that . Doing things to make their life easier or better in some way.	Forgetting the task. Overpromising and underdelivering on your commitments. Putting other people above your child.
Physical Touch	Using non-verbal body language. Being in physical contact with them either in active play or in close connection.	Neglect, avoiding, or refusing physical touch. Hurting physically/ threatening them with a physical consequence.

Communicating in your child's preferred way is the key to reaching their heart and keeping your relationship in Summer. The kind, loving things you do will be recognized as expressions of love and appreciated the most. That means the lines of communication and the threads of connection will strengthen.

CHAPTER 13

Building Great Relationships With the Five Elements of Awareness

....

On *our journey through* the Five Elements of Awareness, we covered a lot of ground:

- We identified our Core Values that consciously and unconsciously shape our perspective. As well, we realized that even though we may have a specific core value from our family of origin, our experiences and our understanding of the world, our values can evolve to bring us closer to who we want to be as parents and people.
- We created our Family Value List, providing us with guidelines that impact where we go, what we focus on, and where we invest our time, money, and energy.
- We created a document for our family priorities and goals, removing some busy-ness and elevating the people, projects, activities and dreams that matter most, and scheduled those items onto our calendars to make sure they happened.

- We identified our child's temperament and realized that their innate styles need to be honored and incorporated into the way our family interacts with each other and with the outside world to feel most connected and successful.
- We discovered which communication strategy our children used the most and developed ways to speak their language to stay connected and in Summer.

Having all of these tools and systems will help us return to Summer and stay in the feelings of connection and love.

But there's one more flower I want to plant in your garden before we part ways.

CHAPTER 14

Growing Together

• • • • • • •

My *dad was a* sailor from Newfoundland.

As a young man, he often sailed off the coast of eastern Canada in the unpredictable Atlantic waters. He saw how powerful and dangerous the ocean could be and he developed a deep respect and love for lighthouses. He knew in every dark, stormy night, the flicker from a lighthouse was all a crew needed to right their course.

I encourage you: look for the lighthouses in your life.

Of course, this book is your forever reference, and I also invite you to tap into your network of family and friends, religious or spiritual teachers, or consult experts, read books of encouragement, or find relevant podcasts or websites.

While all of these are excellent *external* options, I deeply believe that your first step is to simply turn inward.

Search your heart. Ask your higher power to guide you to your next step. In the cold, bleak, blustery Winter season we may need to move forward one itty-bitty step at a time.

Make a slow-and-steady commitment to be deeply connected

to your children even when the days are long because in all honesty, the years are short. Our children grow up and start their own lives in a blink. Investing in a strong, nurturing relationship with them throughout their childhood will give them all they need to make the world a better place.

Final Thoughts

Now that you have experienced the power and possibility of leading your kids with love through *The 5 Seasons of Connection*, you have limitless potential for happiness and joy.

Whichever path you choose when you reach the Crossroads, know that you have all of your experience, intuition, and wisdom to guide you. If you wobble, or if you feel a little ungrounded, return to these practices:

- Commit to knowing and integrating your Personal Core Values and Family Values to stay true to your principles.
- Purposefully and passionately speak in your child's communication style.
- Revisit your goals and priorities. If they are feeling big or burdensome, select new ones so your family finds success.
- Journal about your thoughts, feelings, fears, beliefs, and keep challenging yourself. Are they yours? Or were they handed down from outside sources? What patterns do you see?
- Build self-care practices to fill you with love and increase your overall well-being so you can come to your kids rested

and ready to share your time, talent, and gifts.

- Read everything that takes you deeper into self-awareness.
- Spend time sharing your experiences with amazing friends who also follow *The 5 Seasons of Connection* philosophy.
- Find *The 5 Seasons of Connection* on social media and join our community to find encouragement, inspiration and new ideas.

The purpose of *The 5 Seasons of Connection* is to help you know the seasons of your relationships, recognize when you're slipping into the chilliness of Fall or the dark days of Winter, build a bridge back together in Spring, and celebrate the glow of Summer.

When we learn how to weather the storms on our parenting journey and guide our families back to that safe, happy place, we'll enjoy all the beauty of the season.

Keep in mind that everyday won't be daisies and butterflies. There will be days when we can only meet our kids' basic needs for food, a warm bed, and a quick hug because we are running on fumes. Tell your children you love them. Ask for their grace to allow you time to rest, be alone, and recharge. Know what you need and ask for their help so that you can get it.

In my hundreds of interactions with my kids every week, I don't always get it right. I have practiced these strategies countless times. Be gentle with yourself. Take more time at the Crossroads if you need it. Heck, stay there all day if that grounds you in your inner wisdom! Trust yourself. You are more ready than you think.

Parenting isn't about perfection but about being connected

emotionally, spiritually, and physically. My hope is that armed with this new model for interactions, you'll feel more confident about your parenting. You'll feel connected to your children in ways you've never experienced before.

You now have newfound:

Awareness.
Knowingness.
Hopefulness.
Togetherness.
Belongingness.
Happiness.
Connectedness.

Mastering these new ideas will take time and patience, but your family will thrive with each decision you make towards connection.

We have arrived at the end.

I hope I've served as a lighthouse for your journey. On your stormiest nights, I pray *The 5 Seasons of Connection* help you find your way. Thank you for being on this journey with me! I wish you a lifetime of long, beautiful Summer days.

You are ready to parent with purpose and live with love!

Go confidently in the direction of your dreams.
Live the life you have imagined.

~ Henry David Thoreau,
Philosopher and Poet

Gratitudes

....

I am grateful for you, my new friend. I hope that you find value within these pages to keep you deeply connected in your most important relationships, enjoying many glorious, Summer days.

I am grateful for my sister, Dorothy. She has a limitless capacity to hold space for me, hanging out on the *Leanne Channel* until I'm ready to get up and carry on. She encourages me to keep moving forward, by sprint or by crawl. I never stopped because she believed in me. I love you more than you could imagine!

I am grateful for my mom, Isabelle, and brother, David, for cheering me on. Love you both! And to my dad, who is playing Newfie songs in heaven for me. I miss you.

I am grateful for Katie Cross, my editor, who guided this project from where it was to where it is. Thank you for your support and expertise; I couldn't have done it without you!

I am grateful for my readers who helped me focus on the key messages, especially my dear friends Greta Climer, Mickelle Weary and Karen Bielitz who gave me such important feedback. Thank you!

I am grateful to my friend Gaby Sol who provided loving space for me to expand my understanding of the Universe and create big magic in Amsterdam. Thank you!

I am grateful to Laura Allen, my butt-kicking friend. I couldn't see the summit until you helped me climb through the fog, opening up a world of possibilities for me. Always.

I am grateful to the magical and profound friendships I made at Community School. I chose this elementary school for my kids not knowing it would change the course of *my* life completely. Parents, staff and students, I adore you!

I am grateful for my Seattle-area entrepreneurial sisters in Business Among Moms, Front Seat Life, Girlfriend's Success Circle, and Illuminating Women who encouraged me to reach for the farthest star and hold on tight. And to my dearest, sassiest Seattle sister, Amy Lang. Love ya!

I am grateful to the friendships and support I have found in person at Mompreneurs and Biz Chix, and in the FB groups of League of The Extraordinary and Coffee With Dan.

I am grateful for my new friends at Cruising Writers who called me a *Writer*, cheering for me. Thank you!

I am grateful to my clients who brought The 5 Seasons into their homes to connect in new and exciting ways with their children. My heart bursts with happiness for you!

I am grateful for all the *things* that helped me out: Microsoft Word's Read Aloud that enabled me to close my eyes, hear my words, and notice the holes. Dark chocolate and chamomile tea. My laptop so I could work from every soccer game, dance competition and Fortnite Tournament. Scented candles. Lavender oil. My journal. More chocolate.

Saving the best for last, I am so grateful for my family!

Thank you, Jack, for your love, help and support while I was on this journey of discovering the seasons, bringing them into our family, and then sharing them with the world and all that entailed. I am so thankful for all you do for us!

Without question, my best and brightest Summer days are those spent with my three magnificent kids. There is no scale to measure how deeply and entirely I love and cherish Alex, Nicole and Michael and I am profoundly blessed and eternally honored to be their mom. Just remember cuties, you chose me ;)